Wearable-Tech Projects with the Raspberry Pi Zero

Create imaginative, real-world wearable-tech projects with the Raspberry Pi Zero

Jon Witts

BIRMINGHAM - MUMBAI

Wearable-Tech Projects with the Raspberry Pi Zero

First published: July 2017

Production reference: 1130717

Published by Packt Publishing Ltd.
Livery Place
35 Livery Street
Birmingham
B3 2PB, UK.

ISBN 978-1-78646-881-9

www.packtpub.com

Credits

Author
Jon Witts

Reviewer
David Grainger

Commissioning Editor
Vijin Boricha

Acquisition Editor
Meeta Rajani

Content Development Editor
Devika Battike

Technical Editor
Mohd Riyan Khan

Copy Editor
Yesha Gangani

Project Coordinator
Judie Jose

Proofreader
Safis Editing

Indexer
Rekha Nair

Graphics
Kirk D'Penha

Production Coordinator
Aparna Bhagat

About the Author

Jon Witts has been working within the IT industry since 2001, and specifically within Educational IT since 2004. He was introduced to Linux back in 2001, through his collaboration with two German artists who were visiting the arts organization he was then working with. Having studied both Fine Art and Educational Technology, he has sought to innovate with open and accessible digital technologies within his creative practice. Jon is happiest when deconstructing technology and finding its limits.

Jon has embedded within his school the use of Raspberry Pi computers as an integral part of the delivery of the school's Computer Science curriculum. Being a Raspberry Pi Certified Educator, Jon runs various school clubs and projects, such as a Raspberry Pi Robot Building club. Jon also organizes and runs Raspberry Jam events in the 2017 UK City of Culture, Kingston upon Hull.

This book is dedicated to my three beautiful daughters, Mabel, Ember, and Ada; may you always continue to be as curious about the world as you are and never accept anyone else's limitations!

I would like to thank my wife, Sally, and our three daughters (plus pets!) for putting up with all the cables and components around the house, and not least for being so tolerant of the need to dodge the robots racing round the kitchen floor and avoid the soldering iron when eating breakfast at the table!

I would also like to thank Debbie for her help with some of the trickier textile elements to this book and the amazing Raspberry Pi community for all their help and support with the issues I encountered while planning and building the projects in this book.

About the Reviewer

David Grainger is a teacher of physics and IT since 1999. He is a graduate of physics from The University of Edinburgh and is currently the Head of Physics at Queen Margaret's school.

He has always maintained a passion for using technology and computers. He became a Raspberry Pi Certified Educator in 2015 and started a new Computer Science department.

He is the inaugural graduate of Raspberry Pi's Skycademy program and to date has successfully launched and recovered three Raspberry Pis to approximately 30 km into the stratosphere.

He has used Raspberry Pi to teach computer science to KS3s and ultimately GCSEs.

www.PacktPub.com

For support files and downloads related to your book, please visit www.PacktPub.com.

Did you know that Packt offers eBook versions of every book published, with PDF and ePub files available? You can upgrade to the eBook version at www.PacktPub.com and as a print book customer, you are entitled to a discount on the eBook copy. Get in touch with us at service@packtpub.com for more details.

At www.PacktPub.com, you can also read a collection of free technical articles, sign up for a range of free newsletters and receive exclusive discounts and offers on Packt books and eBooks.

https://www.packtpub.com/mapt

Get the most in-demand software skills with Mapt. Mapt gives you full access to all Packt books and video courses, as well as industry-leading tools to help you plan your personal development and advance your career.

Why subscribe?

- Fully searchable across every book published by Packt
- Copy and paste, print, and bookmark content
- On demand and accessible via a web browser

Customer Feedback

Thanks for purchasing this Packt book. At Packt, quality is at the heart of our editorial process. To help us improve, please leave us an honest review on this book's Amazon page at `http://www.amazon.com/dp/1786468816`.

If you'd like to join our team of regular reviewers, you can e-mail us at `customerreviews@packtpub.com`. We award our regular reviewers with free eBooks and videos in exchange for their valuable feedback. Help us be relentless in improving our products!

Table of Contents

Preface

Are you interested in wearable-tech and gadgets? Do you want to know more about how you can use the Raspberry Pi Zero computer? This book has a series of projects which will show you some of the possibilities with wearable-tech and the Pi Zero, guiding you through each one from start to finish.

The Raspberry Pi Zero is a revolutionary product, designed and manufactured in the United Kingdom by the Raspberry Pi Foundation. This tiny computer provides powerful features, in spite of being such a small size; it measures a mere 65 x 35 mm! One of the advantages of its tiny size is that it is ideal to be used in wearable-tech projects.

You will begin at the beginning (as all good journeys do!) and learn how to install the required software for your upcoming projects. You will also learn how to control electronic devices with the GPIOZero Python library. Next, you will be creating some stylish wearable-tech projects such as a motion-reactive LED cap and Tweet-activated LED T-shirt. Towards the end of the book, you will be creating some useful health and fitness wearable-tech projects; these will help you monitor your heart-rate, track your movements with GPS, and count your footsteps with your own pedometer.

By the end of the book, you will have created a range of wearable-tech projects and learned enough about your Raspberry Pi Zero that you should be able to adapt these projects further or come up with your own creations!

What this book covers

Chapter 1, *About the Raspberry Pi*. This chapter introduces the Raspberry Pi Zero computer that we will be using throughout the book; it explains how to get the required software installed and running. We will look at how we can connect to our Pi Zero over SSH from a remote computer so we can program it without having to attach a monitor, keyboard or mouse. We will then look at how we can control basic electronic devices using the Python GPIOZero library. Finally, we will wire up an 'off switch' to our Pi Zero, so that when it is running headless in our later projects, we can safely power it 'off'.

Chapter 2, *Scrolling LED Badge*. In this chapter we will make a scrolling LED badge that you can program to display any message across and can be worn while out and about. We will make use of the Scroll pHAT HD from Pimoroni and our Pi Zero to create your badge. We will also look at how we can incorporate a battery pack to make this a portable solution. We will use Python to program our Scroll pHAT HD to display whatever message we want. Finally, we will look at ensuring this program runs as soon as we turn on our Pi Zero.

Chapter 3, *Sewable LEDs in Clothing*. This chapter uses stitchable LEDs and conductive thread to transform an item of clothing into a sparkling LED piece of wearable-tech, controlled with a Pi Zero hidden in the item of clothing. We will incorporate a Pi Zero and battery into a hidden pocket in the garment and connect our stitchable LEDs to the Pis GPIO pins so that we can write a Python program to control the order and timings of the LEDs.

Chapter 4, *A Motion-Reactive LED Cap*. In this chapter we will make use of a Pimoroni Blinkt LED strip, an Adafruit Triple-Axis Accelerometer and a Pi Zero to create a cap with a super-bright strip of RGB LEDs across the front. This will change its colors and display pattern, based upon the direction and speed that the wearer moves.

Chapter 5, *A Tweet activated LED T-shirt*. This project shows us how to incorporate some LEDs into another item of clothing, a t-shirt or jumper, and again wire them back to a hidden Pi Zero and battery pack. With our Pi Zero connected to a Wi-Fi network, we will then write a program, which monitors Twitter and listens out for trigger phrases. Whenever these trigger phrases are detected, our LEDs will light up in the different patterns we have programmed them to.

Chapter 6, *An LED Laptop bag*. Here we will cut and resolder an Adafruit DotStar Strip into a matrix of super-bright, controllable RGB LEDs. We will then attach this matrix to the front of a laptop bag. Next, we will hide our Pi Zero and battery pack inside the pocket of the bag and write the Python program to control our RGB LED matrix.

Chapter 7, *Create Your Own pedometer*. In this chapter we will make use of an Adafruit Triple-Axis Accelerometer, a Pimoroni Scroll pHAT HD, and a Pi Zero to create our own pedometer. Once we have connected the accelerometer and Scroll pHAT HD to the Pi Zero, we will write the program, which reads the data from the accelerometer and converts it into steps taken. We will then complete our program to make it display the updating step count on the Scroll pHAT HD.

Chapter 8, *Create Your Own Heart Rate Monitor*. With this project, we will use a Pulse Sensor Amped to create our own heart rate monitor device. We will add a Pimoroni Enviro pHAT and a Scroll pHAT HD to enable us to read the sensor data and display an animation of a heart beating in time with ours. As well as this, the device will display our heart's current BPM on the Scroll pHAT HD.

Chapter 9, *Create Your Own GPS Tracker*. Our final chapter will see us create a portable GPS tracker for bikers, runners or walkers to use when out and about. The GPS tracker will log your GPS coordinates, including elevation and time. We will also configure the Pi to create a file in the correct format for you to import into Google Maps or Google Earth to plot the course you have taken.

What you will need

The required hardware for each project is mentioned right at the beginning of every chapter; all software that is used in these projects is Open Source and freely available from the Internet. You will need a Raspberry Pi Zero of course; the latest Pi Zero W is recommended, so that you can make use of the on-board Wi-Fi to access your computer remotely without the need for an additional USB Wi-Fi dongle.

You will also need access to various tools for the different projects in this book. Again, each chapter details what you will need; the essential 'shopping list' includes a soldering iron, wire strippers, and a set of crocodile-clip helping hands.

Who this book is for

Everyone.

While some prior knowledge of Python programming and use of the terminal on the Raspberry Pi would be advantageous, they are by no means necessary. Each chapter clearly sets the steps to be taken on your wearable-tech adventure. Chapter 1, *About the Raspberry Pi*, assumes no prior knowledge to get your Pi Zero and you up and running. The complexity of the electronic devices used progress incrementally as you work through the chapters; there are clear steps to follow and pictures to help you at every turn along the way.

Conventions

In this book, you will find a number of text styles that distinguish between different kinds of information. Here are some examples of these styles and an explanation of their meaning. Code words in text, database table names, folder names, filenames, file extensions, path names, dummy URLs, user input, and Twitter handles are shown as follows: "We start a `while True:` loop, which will continue until we stop the program." A block of code is set as follows:

```
def adxlToRGB(axis):
    axes = adxl345.getAxes(True)
    absADXL = abs(axes[axis])
    if (absADXL >= 1):
        absADXL = 1
    rgbADXL = int(255 * absADXL)
    return rgbADXL
```

When we wish to draw your attention to a particular part of a code block, the relevant lines or items are set in bold:

```
def adxlToRGB(axis):
    axes = adxl345.getAxes(True)
    absADXL = abs(axes[axis])
    if (absADXL >= 1):
        absADXL = 1
    rgbADXL = int(255 * absADXL)
    return rgbADXL
```

Any command-line input or output is written as follows:

```
sudo nano /lib/systemd/system/wearableHat.service
```

New terms and **important words** are shown in bold. Words that you see on the screen, for example, in menus or dialog boxes, appear in the text like this: "Click on the blue **Select image** button and browse to the Jessie Lite zip archive you just downloaded"

Warnings or important notes appear like this.

Tips and tricks appear like this.

Reader feedback

Feedback from our readers is always welcome. Let us know what you think about this book-what you liked or disliked. Reader feedback is important for us as it helps us develop titles that you will really get the most out of. To send us general feedback, simply e-mail `feedback@packtpub.com`, and mention the book's title in the subject of your message. If there is a topic that you have expertise in and you are interested in either writing or contributing to a book, see our author guide at `www.packtpub.com/authors`.

Customer support

Now that you are the proud owner of a Packt book, we have a number of things to help you to get the most from your purchase.

Downloading the example code

You can download the example code files for this book from your account at `http://www.packtpub.com`. If you purchased this book elsewhere, you can visit `http://www.packtpub.com/support` and register to have the files e-mailed directly to you. You can download the code files by following these steps:

1. Log in or register to our website using your e-mail address and password.
2. Hover the mouse pointer on the **SUPPORT** tab at the top.
3. Click on **Code Downloads & Errata**.
4. Enter the name of the book in the **Search** box.
5. Select the book for which you're looking to download the code files.
6. Choose from the drop-down menu where you purchased this book from.
7. Click on **Code Download**.

Once the file is downloaded, please make sure that you unzip or extract the folder using the latest version of:

- WinRAR / 7-Zip for Windows
- Zipeg / iZip / UnRarX for Mac
- 7-Zip / PeaZip for Linux

The code bundle for the book is also hosted on GitHub at: `https://github.com/PacktPubl ishing/Wearable-Tech-Projects-with-the-Raspberry-Pi-Zero`. We also have other code bundles from our rich catalog of books and videos available at: `https://github.com /PacktPublishing/`. Check them out!

Downloading the color images of this book

We also provide you with a PDF file that has color images of the screenshots/diagrams used in this book. The color images will help you better understand the changes in the output. You can download this file from `https://www.packtpub.com/sites/default/files/down loads/WearableTechProjectswiththeRaspberryPiZero_ColorImages.pdf`.

Errata

Although we have taken every care to ensure the accuracy of our content, mistakes do happen. If you find a mistake in one of our books-maybe a mistake in the text or the code-we would be grateful if you could report this to us. By doing so, you can save other readers from frustration and help us improve subsequent versions of this book. If you find any errata, please report them by visiting `http://www.packtpub.com/submit-errata`, selecting your book, clicking on the **Errata Submission Form** link, and entering the details of your errata. Once your errata are verified, your submission will be accepted and the errata will be uploaded to our website or added to any list of existing errata under the Errata section of that title. To view the previously submitted errata, go to `https://www.packtpub.com/book s/content/support`and enter the name of the book in the search field. The required information will appear under the **Errata** section.

Piracy

Piracy of copyrighted material on the Internet is an ongoing problem across all media. At Packt, we take the protection of our copyright and licenses very seriously. If you come across any illegal copies of our works in any form on the Internet, please provide us with the location address or website name immediately so that we can pursue a remedy. Please contact us at `copyright@packtpub.com` with a link to the suspected pirated material. We appreciate your help in protecting our authors and our ability to bring you valuable content.

Questions

If you have a problem with any aspect of this book, you can contact us at `questions@packtpub.com`, and we will do our best to address the problem.

1
About the Raspberry Pi

Throughout this book, we will be making use of the Raspberry Pi Zero computer to create our wearable-tech projects. However, before we jump straight into our first project, we should first some time getting to know the Raspberry Pi Zero computer and performing a few basic tasks, which will be useful across all of our projects. We will first look at the history of this tiny computer, and then learn how to get our software up and running, along with connecting to the GPIO headers on our computer. We will then spend some time looking at the different ways we can access our computer when it is not connected to a keyboard, mouse, or monitor and also perform some basic electronics experiments to get to know how we can use the GPIO pins in our upcoming projects.

So, let's get started!

What we will cover

In this chapter, we will cover the following topics:

- The history of the Raspberry Pi Zero
- The parts we will need to complete this chapter
- Installing our operating system onto our Pi Zero
- Different ways of connecting to our GPIO headers on our PI Zero
- Accessing our Pi Zero in headless mode
- Creating a very basic electronics project to familiarize ourselves with using GPIO pins on our Pi

A little history

Raspberry Pi Foundation launched the Raspberry Pi Zero on 26th November 2015, taking the IT world by surprise by releasing it secretly at a price of just $5, along with including a free Raspberry Pi Zero for those who were lucky enough to get a copy of that month's *MagPie* magazine. Needless to say, these tiny computers sold out quickly and, to this day, customers are still limited to purchasing just one device per order from the suppliers who stock them.

In April 2016, a new version of the Pi Zero was launched; a camera port was added to this model, enabling enthusiasts to build super small camera projects and hacks using their Raspberry Pi Zero computers.

The newest and latest version of Raspberry Pi Zero is Pi Zero W. It adds to the second generation of Pi Zero by now including the same Wi-Fi and Bluetooth on-board chip, which was introduced on Pi 3. This makes Pi Zero W a great choice of computer for our projects in this book; it has enough power to deliver what we want, and GPIO pins allow us to connect to and control all manner of devices (as we will see!); and we now have a means to connect to this computer, while it is hidden away in a piece of clothing!

With this in mind, I will be making use of Pi Zero W for all of the projects in this book. If you cannot get your hands on one, don't worry; all these projects will work fine with any Raspberry Pi computer from the model B+ upwards.

The bill of parts

We will make use of the following things in this project:

- A Pi Zero W computer
- A micro SD card (8 GB minimum)
- A GPIO header set (optional)
- Another computer or a laptop with an SD card writer
- Internet access
- A soldering iron and solder
- Some Blu-Tack (or similar substance)
- One red and one green 5 mm LED
- Two 330 Ω resistors
- A push type button
- Some red and black sheathed cable

Installing our software

Throughout all the projects of this book, we are going to make use of the Raspbian operating system. More specifically, we will be using the Jessie Lite version of this operating system. Raspbian is the foundation's officially supported operating system and the one for which there is most community support for. It is derived from the Debian Linux operating system; so if you have used that or any of its derivatives (like Ubuntu) before, you should feel at home with Raspbian. I have decided to go with the Jessie Lite version of Raspbian for a couple of reasons:

1. All of our projects will run headless (without a monitor, keyboard, or mouse), so why have a display manager use up our resources?
2. The lower footprint of this operating system, in terms of memory and storage usage, will give us access to more of the computer's resources to use for our projects.

So, head over to `https://www.raspberrypi.org/downloads/raspbian/` and download the latest version of the Jessie Lite operating system. Once this ZIP archive is downloaded on your computer, you will need to copy it onto your micro SD card.

Using Etcher to copy our image

Until recently, there was a different way to copy an image file to an SD card in every different operating system; the open source piece of software, Etcher, sets out to solve this problem. Etcher is freely available for pretty much all operating systems, so we only need to document one process for all operating systems rather than detailing a different method for each OS. Etcher will run on any operating system that can run Electron. You can check the full list of supported operating systems for Electron on their website at `http://electron.a tom.io/docs/tutorial/supported-platforms/`.

 Etcher is only supported in macOS version 10.9 and higher, so if you are running a lower version of macOS, you can find other ways to install the image file on your SD card over on the Raspberry Pi site at `https://www.r aspberrypi.org/documentation/installation/installing-images/ma c.md`; you should also probably consider getting your version of macOS upgraded too!

So, to get started with Etcher, head over to their website at `https://etcher.io` and download the latest version for your operating system. Run the installer as per the standard method for your operating system.

Once you have Etcher installed, open it and you should be presented with a screen like the following screenshot:

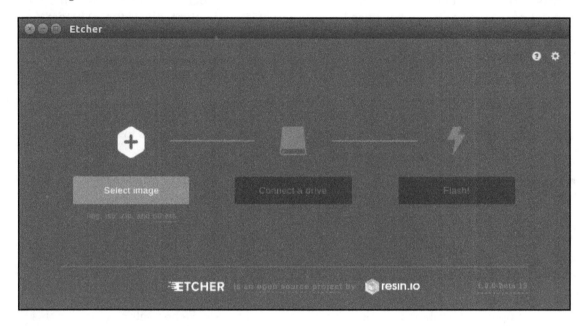

Click on the blue **Select image** button and browse to the Jessie Lite ZIP archive you just downloaded; there is no need to extract the ZIP archive with Etcher. You will then be presented with a screen like this:

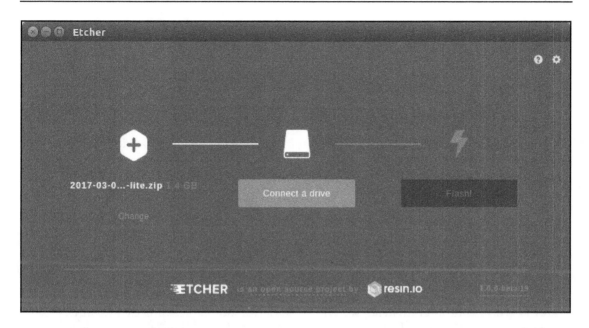

At this point, you should insert your SD card into your computer's SD card reader. Etcher should automatically detect your SD card and progress onto the third section of the process. Click on the blue **Flash!** button to begin the copying process, and Etcher should display something similar to this:

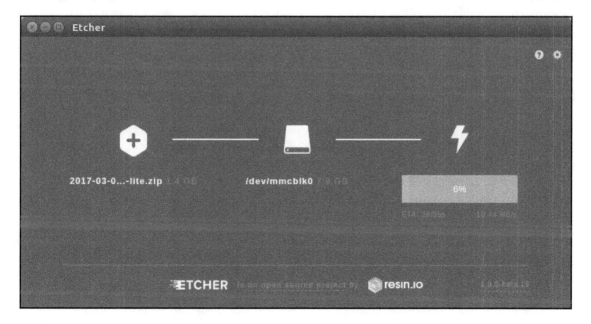

If you are prompted to provide administrative credentials for Etcher to flash your SD card, then enter the required credentials and allow Etcher to complete.

You will be shown a completion estimate, the percentage copied, and the transfer rate in the Etcher window. Allow Etcher to complete this; then exit the program; and remove your SD card from your computer (no need to safely remove or eject it, Etcher has done it for you!).

You have now copied Raspbian Jessie Lite to your SD card, and you're ready to move on to our next section, *Connecting to the GPIO headers*.

Connecting to GPIO headers

For many of our projects, as we will be trying to make them as small as possible, we will probably not make use of the standard GPIO headers, which you most likely received with your Pi Zero W computer. Instead, we will be soldering our cables directly into our Pi Zero W. If you prefer to just test these projects out and would like to reuse your Pi Zero W for other projects, then it will probably make sense to sacrifice a bit of space and attach the GPIO headers to your Pi Zero W. Until recently, you only had one option to do this; solder the headers to your computer! This involves a steady hand, a keen eye, and some patience. I will talk you through this, as we are going to need to solder for many of the projects in this book; so it is a valuable skill to have even if you don't use it to attach headers to your Pi Zero. If the idea of soldering 40 very closely spaced pins onto your Pi Zero fills you with dread, you now have another option; many of the online stores stocking Raspberry Pi components now stock what are known as **hammer headers**. These allow you t attach the 40 small pins to the GPIO pins of your Pi Zero using only a hammer; no soldering required!

Hammer headers

You can purchase new hammer headers from a number of different retailers. Both Pimoroni (`https://shop.pimoroni.com`) and Pi Hut (`https://thepihut.com`) have them listed, and both companies ship to a wide range of countries.

 If you choose to use the hammer headers, please ensure that you follow all of the instructions from the supplier or you risk irreparably damaging your Raspberry Pi computer!

Solder headers

The more traditional method of attaching your GPIO headers, and the one I have always used, is to solder them to the board. As I mentioned earlier, for most of the projects, I will not attach the header blocks in this manner and will just solder directly to the board; however, this is a skill worth learning, and some of the add-on cards or hats we will be using will require us to attach the headers before we can use them.

I include this section more for completeness about setting up a Raspberry Pi Zero, but as you will see in the projects in this book, I will be soldering our components directly to the Pi Zero and not making use of header pins. If you choose to solder the headers to your Pi Zero, then you will be able to follow the projects in the book by soldering to your header pins rather than directly doing so to the Pi.

Getting your equipment ready

You will need a soldering iron, some solder, and a blob of fixative such as Blu-Tack for this. I tend to always use leaded solder, as I find that it melts quicker and gives a better solder joint than unleaded solder, but the choice is yours.

Plug your iron in and allow it to come up to temperature. Once your iron is hot enough, apply a little solder to the tip. This is known as tinning your tip, and it fills any imperfections in your iron's tip with solder. This gives a better transfer of heat between the tip of your iron and the components your are soldering.

Now, insert the header into the Pi Zero and turn it upside down so that it is resting on the header pins evenly across the length of the Pi Zero. Then, place a blob of Blu-Tack under the side of the Pi Zero opposite the header pins, just enough to hold it flat while you begin to solder the pins, as shown here:

Now, we can begin to solder the pins to the Pi Zero; we are aiming for a nice, conical solder joint that just covers the brass ring around the hole in the Pi Zero board and comes to a point at the top of the pin. Place the tip of your soldering iron so that it touches both the brass ring on the board and the metal of the pin you are soldering, but nothing else, as shown next. Leave it for a few seconds to heat both brass ring and pin, and then apply the solder to the joint. The solder should melt, and you should see it flow into the hole and cover the brass and the pin. After a few seconds, remove the solder, and then remove your iron. Leave the joint to cool for a few seconds, and then move on to the next.

I tend to work my way down one side of the header and then rotate the Pi and solder the other side. The following picture shows what a finished soldered header should look like:

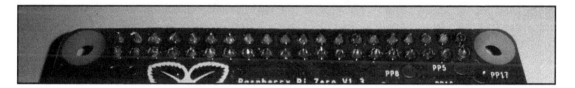

Headless access

For all of the projects in this book, we will not be connecting directly to our Pi, as it will be installed into various different objects and will need to run without a keyboard, mouse, or monitor attached. This is known as running a computer *headless*. To effectively do this, we need a method to connect to our Pi remotely so that we can perform the programming we need to do without having to attach bulky devices to it. This is where Pi Zero W really comes into its own; the integrated Wi-Fi means that we can connect to the Pi over a Wi-Fi network without having to add any additional hardware.

If you are using a Raspberry Pi other than Pi Zero W or Pi 3, then you will need to add a Wi-Fi dongle to your Pi to be able to connect to it remotely. If it is a Pi Zero 1.1 or 1.3 that you are using, then you will also need a USB micro shim as shown here. You can pick these up for a few pounds from many online retailers:

There are a couple of things we will need to do to get our Raspberry Pi SD card ready for remote access; fortunately the Raspberry Pi Foundation has tried to make these as straightforward as possible for us.

Enabling SSH access

We are going to use **Secure Shell** (**SSH**) to remotely connect to our Pi. As the default password of the Raspberry Pi Raspbian OS is well known, and as more and more *Internet of Things* devices are being made with the Raspberry Pi computers, the decision was made by the Raspberry Pi Foundation that SSH should be disabled by default, requiring a user to select to turn it on before its first use. If you are running your Pi connected to a keyboard and monitor, then this is easily done by making use of the `raspi-config` utility. The Foundation has also given us a way to enable SSH for those running their Raspberry Pi computers in headless mode.

To turn on SSH for a Pi that you are going to run headless, all you need to do is create an empty file (with no file extension) named SSH on the boot partition of your Pi's SD card. When you first boot your Raspberry Pi, SSH will then be enabled and the file removed from the boot partition of the SD card. As the boot partition is a FAT32 formatted partition, it can be read from and written to by any operating system. More details can be found on the official Raspberry Pi documentation: `https://www.raspberrypi.org/documentation/rem ote-access/ssh/`

Setting up your Wi-Fi network

To be able to connect to our Raspberry Pi Zero, we are going to need a working network connection. We will be using the Pi Zero W's Wi-Fi network for this. If you are using a Pi without built-in Wi-Fi, then these instructions will still work, you will just need to connect a USB Wi-Fi dongle to your Pi first.

We have been given a straightforward method of configuring our Wi-Fi connection when using our Pi in headless mode too. If we create a file called `wpa_supplicant.conf` in the boot partition of our Pi's SD card, upon first boot, this file is copied into the `/etc/wpa_supplicant/` directory and used to configure the Wi-Fi settings for the Pi. However, this file must contain a valid set of configuration details, or your Pi will not connect to your Wi-Fi.

Here is an example of a `wpa_supplicant.conf` file setup to connect to the Wi-Fi network called `mywifinetwork` with a connection password of `mypassword`. You should obviously change these to match the details of your Wi-Fi network when writing your file. You can read more about the different configurations you can add to this file over at the Raspberry Pi's official documentation pages at `https://www.raspberrypi.org/documentation/conf iguration/wireless/wireless-cli.md`:

```
network={
    ssid="mywifinetwork"
    psk="mypassword"
}
```

It is worth double checking the format and details entered here, as any mistakes in this file will stop your Pi Zero from joining your wireless network.

Connecting to your Pi

Now that we have set up SSH access and our Wi-Fi network, we can start up our Pi Zero and connect to it from another computer remotely. As we are using the Jessie Lite version of Raspbian; there is no X-server to provide a desktop, therefore VNC connections are not an option. How you connect to your Pi using SSH will depend upon which operating system you are using for your computer or laptop. Once you have established a SSH connection, the steps for each future project are the same regardless of the operating system your computer is running.

Insert your SD card you previously prepared into your Pi Zero and then connect a micro USB power supply to the port labelled **PWR**, as shown in the following picture. All being well, you should see the green activity LED flashing as your Pi Zero boots up for the first time.

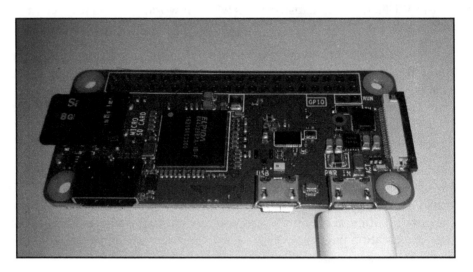

However, before we can begin to connect, you will need to discover the IP address that your Wi-Fi network has assigned to your Pi. There are a number of different ways of doing this, and the way which works for you will largely depend upon your network. The method that I usually use at home, is to connect to my home router's web interface and view the **Attached Devices** page. This will be different for each router and may or may not exist! My router page looks like the next picture. By default, your Raspberry Pi will show up with the host-name of **RASPBERRYPI**. You can change this once you get the remote access to the Pi. If you can not find out DHCP address leases from your router in this manner, then the Raspberry Pi documentation has some other methods that you can use to find the IP address of your headless Pi at https://www.raspberrypi.org/documentation/remote-access/ip-address.md:

Attached Devices				

Access Control: Turned Off

Go to <u>Access Control</u> to allow or block devices.

Refresh

Wired Devices

#	Device Name	IP Address	MAC Address	Connection Type
1				wired
2				wired

2.4GHz Wireless Devices (Wireless Intruders also show up here)

#	Device Name	IP Address	MAC Address	Connection Type
1				wireless
2				wireless
3	RASPBERRYPI	192.168.1.61	B8:27:EB	wireless
4				wireless
5				wireless

5GHz Wireless Devices (Wireless Intruders also show up here)

#	Device Name	IP Address	MAC Address	Connection Type
1				
2				

You can see that on my router, my Pi Zero has been assigned an IP address of `192.168.1.61`. Now, we know the IP address of our Pi, we can access it from our other computer or laptop.

 When connecting to a host via SSH for the first time, it is normal to be warned that the authenticity of the host can not be established. If you get this warning after you have connected to a device previously, this could indicate that your SSH connection is being intercepted, or someone has changed the SSH keys on your Pi!

SSH from Windows

To connect to your Pi Zero using SSH from the a Windows operating system, you will need to download a small tool called *PuTTY*. This is freely available at `http://www.chiark.gree nend.org.uk/~sgtatham/putty/latest.html`. Download either the 32 bit or 64 bit installer, whichever is appropriate to your Windows system, and then run the installer.

Once installed, run PuTTY and enter the IP address of your Raspberry Pi into the **Host Name** field and click on **Open**, as shown in the following screenshot:

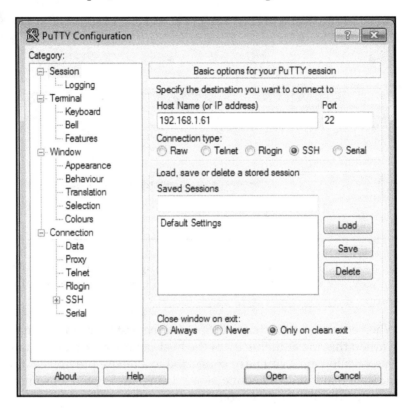

As this is your first time connecting to your Pi Zero over SSH with this PuTTY install, you will be presented with a **PuTTY Security Alert** window about the server's host key not being cached. This is normal, so just click on **Yes**. A terminal window will then open and ask you to log in. Enter `pi` for the username and `raspberry` for the password. You will then be logged in to your Pi remotely. You can now move on to the *Final setup* section.

Highlighting any text with your mouse in the PuTTY terminal window copies it to your Windows clipboard, and right-clicking on the PuTTY terminal window pastes the contents of your Windows clipboard into PuTTY.

SSH from macOS

To connect to your Pi Zero using SSH from the macOS operating system, you will need to use the Terminal application. You can locate this by opening finder and going to **Applications** and then opening the **Utilities** folder. Once you have located the Terminal application, double-click on it to open it. Enter the following command to connect to your Pi Zero via SSH:

```
ssh pi@192.168.1.61
```

You need to change the IP address in this code to match the IP your Pi has been assigned. You will then be presented with a warning, The authenticity of host '192.168.1.61' can't be established...—this is normal when you connect to a host for the first time over SSH, and you can safely type yes to continue connecting.

You will now be prompted to enter the password; type raspberry and press *Enter*. You are now connected to your Pi Zero via SSH and can move on to the *Final setup* section of this chapter.

SSH from Linux

To connect to your Pi Zero using SSH from a Linux operating system, you will need to use your system Terminal. Type the following command:

```
ssh pi@192.168.1.61
```

You should obviously replace the IP address with the IP address that your Pi has been assigned. As this is the first time you are connecting to your Pi over SSH from your computer, you will be asked whether you want to accept the ECDSA key fingerprint. This is normal on a first connection and nothing to worry about. Type yes and press *Enter* to continue connecting. You will then be prompted to enter the password for your Pi. Enter the default password of raspberry and press *Enter*.

 When you type your password, you will not be shown any asterisks to indicate how many characters you have typed; type carefully!

You are now logged into your Pi Zero via SSH, move on to the *Final Set up* section of this chapter, to get your Pi ready to be used to start making our wearable-tech projects!

Final setup

Now that we have a remote connection to our Pi Zero, there are a few final setup steps to carry out so we are ready to start looking at our projects. The first thing we are going to do is to change our password to access our Pi. The default password is well known, and it is not a good idea to leave any password set as its default. Secondly, we will change the hostname of our Pi so that it is easily recognizable on our network as our Pi for these projects. Finally, we will install some of the basic software packages we are going to need for the projects in this book and also ensure that the other software already installed on the Pi is up-to-date.

Changing your password

To change your password, enter the following command into your SSH connection:

passwd

You will be asked to enter your current password (`raspberry`) and then asked to enter a new password twice. All being well, you should see a message like the one in the next screenshot. After changing a password over an SSH connection, I always open another SSH connection to my Pi and check whether I can successfully connect using my new password before I close the connection:

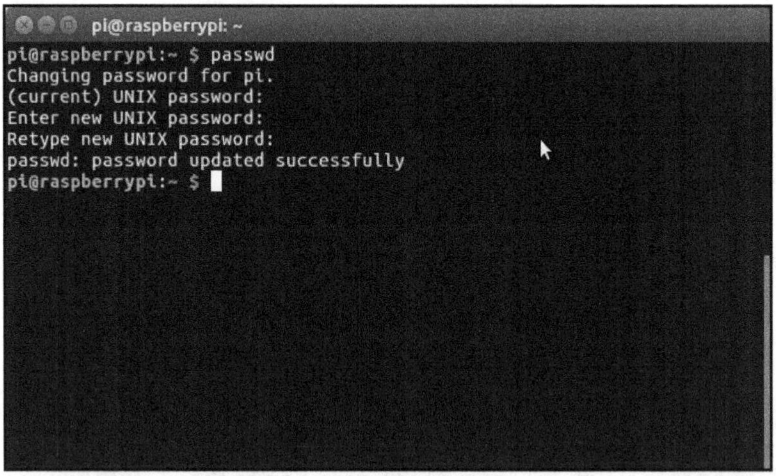

Changing the hour hostname

To change the hostname of our Pi Zero, we are going to make use of the `raspi-config` tool. Type the following command into your SSH connection:

```
sudo raspi-config
```

This will bring up the following menu:

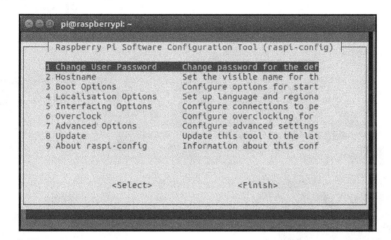

Select option **2** using your cursor keys and press *Enter* to select it. Read and take note of the rules for allowed hostnames, and press *Enter* to select your new hostname. I am calling mine `wearablepi`. Once you have entered your new hostname, press *Enter* to save it. Press your *Tab* key twice to select **<Finish>** on the `raspi-config` menu and press *Enter* to close `raspi-config`. You will be prompted to reboot your Pi Zero. Press *Enter* with **<Yes>** selected, and your Pi Zero will reboot.

When your Pi Zero reboots, it should now show on your router's **Attached Devices** list, with its new hostname.

Reconnect to your Pi Zero via SSH and move onto the next section.

Downloading the example code

Detailed steps to download the code bundle are mentioned in the Preface of this book. The code bundle for the book is also hosted on GitHub at: `htt ps://github.com/PacktPublishing/Wearable-Tech-Projects-with-th e-Raspberry-Pi-Zero`. We also have other code bundles from our rich catalog of books and videos available at: `https://github.com/PacktPubl ishing/`. Check them out!

Installing basic software

We now need to update our existing software and install a few more bits of software ready for our projects. To update our existing software, type the following command into your Pi Zero:

```
sudo apt-get update
```

You should see multiple lines of information appear across your SSH connection, as your Pi Zero updates its information about what software packages are available to it:

```
pi@wearablepi: ~
Get:1 http://archive.raspberrypi.org jessie InRelease [22.9 kB]
Get:2 http://mirrordirector.raspbian.org jessie InRelease [14.9 kB]
Get:3 http://archive.raspberrypi.org jessie/main armhf Packages [147 kB]
Get:4 http://mirrordirector.raspbian.org jessie/main armhf Packages [8,981 kB]
Get:5 http://archive.raspberrypi.org jessie/ui armhf Packages [57.6 kB]
Ign http://archive.raspberrypi.org jessie/main Translation-en_GB
Ign http://archive.raspberrypi.org jessie/main Translation-en
Ign http://archive.raspberrypi.org jessie/ui Translation-en_GB
Ign http://archive.raspberrypi.org jessie/ui Translation-en
Get:6 http://mirrordirector.raspbian.org jessie/contrib armhf Packages [37.5 kB]
Get:7 http://mirrordirector.raspbian.org jessie/non-free armhf Packages [70.3 kB
]
Get:8 http://mirrordirector.raspbian.org jessie/rpi armhf Packages [1,356 B]
Ign http://mirrordirector.raspbian.org jessie/contrib Translation-en_GB
Ign http://mirrordirector.raspbian.org jessie/contrib Translation-en
Ign http://mirrordirector.raspbian.org jessie/main Translation-en_GB
Ign http://mirrordirector.raspbian.org jessie/main Translation-en
Ign http://mirrordirector.raspbian.org jessie/non-free Translation-en_GB
Ign http://mirrordirector.raspbian.org jessie/non-free Translation-en
Ign http://mirrordirector.raspbian.org jessie/rpi Translation-en_GB
Ign http://mirrordirector.raspbian.org jessie/rpi Translation-en
Fetched 9,333 kB in 31s (294 kB/s)
Reading package lists... Done
pi@wearablepi:~ $
```

To upgrade your existing software packages, type the following command:

```
sudo apt-get dist-upgrade
```

This command will make your Pi Zero check to see whether there are any updated software packages available for you to install. If there are, it will ask you to confirm. If prompted to, press *Y* to install your updates and wait for the process to complete.

We are now going to install a couple of new pieces of software, which do not come as standard on the Jessie Lite image, but this we will need for our projects. Type the following code to install the required software:

```
sudo apt-get install python3 python3-gpiozero python3-pip
```

Your Pi Zero will then calculate all the other packages it needs to install to get these three pieces of software working. Enter Y and press *Enter* to begin the installation process. Installing new software and updates on a Pi Zero can take some time, but be patient and it will finish soon enough!

Once this completes, we now have the basic software we need to start on our projects.

Basic electronics

In this section, we will wire up a simple push button, LEDs, resistors to our Pi Zero, and then write some simple Python code that will respond to a user pushing the button and making our LEDs flash.

Wiring up the electronics

We need to wire up our electronic parts, as shown in the following image:

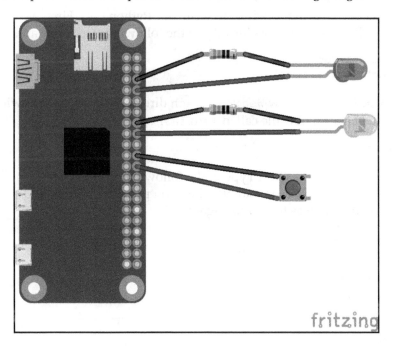

Make sure that your Pi Zero is switched off when you are soldering the cables to the Pi or the header pins! You will also need to take care when wiring your LEDs, as we must get the correct legs attached to the positive and negative wires in our circuit, or they will not work. The positive leg of an LED is usually longer, and there is often a flat edge on the LED to indicate which is the negative leg. We are also going to introduce a 330 Ω resistor between the LED and the ground of the Pi; this is done to stop the LED drawing too much current from the Pi and damaging it.

You may want to introduce a little electrical insulating tape around one leg of each LED to ensure that they do not short circuit by touching the other leg. Once you have soldered your components together, give them a final check over to make sure they are in the correct GPIO holes on the Pi and that you have a good connection at each joint.

Now that we have completed the wiring of our electronics, we can move on to writing the code to control it all. Plug in your Pi and establish a SSH connection to it.

Writing the Python program

We will make use of the *Nano* text editor to write our Python files. First, we will create a directory to save all of our programs into. Type the following two commands:

```
mkdir ~/WearableTech
cd ~/WearableTech
```

We should now be inside our new WearableTech directory. Type the following command to open Nano, and create a new file called ledflash.py:

```
nano ledflash.py
```

We are now in the Nano text editor. Type in the following code to create a simple program, which will make the LEDs flash on and off when you press the button, and then stop the LEDs flashing when you press the button again:

```
#!/usr/bin/python3
from gpiozero import LED, Button

btn = Button(25)
green = LED(23)
red = LED(14)

while True:
    btn.wait_for_press()
    green.blink(0.5,0.5)
    red.blink(0.25,0.25)
```

```
btn.wait_for_press()
green.off()
red.off()
```

Save the file by pressing *Ctrl* and *O* together, followed by the *Enter* key, and then exit Nano by pressing *Ctrl* and *X* together. We are now going to make the file executable by typing the following command:

```
sudo chmod +x ./ledflash.py
```

We can now run the file by typing this:

```
./ledflash.py
```

All being well, you should now be able to press the button wired up to your Pi and LEDs should start blinking at different rates. Press the button again (you may need to hold it for half a second) and your LEDs should switch off! If it doesn't work, check your program and double check your wiring.

If you want to stop your program from running, press *Ctrl* and *C* together.

Breaking down the program

The first line of the program is what is known as a **shebang**. The hash symbol followed by an exclamation mark (#!) tells the computer that what follows the exclamation mark is the details of what the program or interpreter should be used to run the rest of the program. In our case, this is python3, which is located inside the /usr/bin directories. Next, we import two things from the gpiozero library, Button and LED.

The next section of the code deals with setting up our devices. We create a variable, called btn, and tell Python that it is a gpiozero library's Button attached to GPIO pin number 25. We then create a variable for each LED and tell Python that they are gpiozero LEDs attached to pins 23 and 14.

Now, we enter the main part of the program. We start a while loop and just pass True as our condition to the loop; this will mean that this loop never ends (unless you close the program by pressing *Ctrl* and *C* together).

Now, we instruct Python to wait until it detects a press of the button. When it detects a press, we move on to the next line of the program. Here, we set each LED to blink on and off at different rates. The blink class of the `gpiozero` LED defaults to running the blink as a background thread; this means that the blink starts, and then we move onto the next line of code with the blink still running. So, with both LEDs blinking away, we wait again for a button press. When this is detected, we turn off each LED, and then return to the beginning of the loop.

Play around with the program and have a read of what else you can do using the `gpiozero` library on the documentation pages at `https://gpiozero.readthedocs.io/en/stable/`.

In the next chapter, we will get straight into a wearable-tech project using many of the things we have done in this chapter. At this point, you can shut down your Pi and desolder the six cables from it if you like; we will be using some different hardware for the next project!

Summary

In this chapter, you have learned a little bit about the history of Raspberry Pi Zero as well as how to set up Pi Zero from the scratch, including installing the operating system on our SD card and setting up remote access to it for our network.

We then spent some time creating a simple electronic project to get comfortable with some electronics we will be using, along with some of the Python libraries we will be using to control them.

2
Scrolling LED Badge

In our first full project, we are going to make ourselves a badge that connects back to our Pi Zero. The badge itself will be made from a board, which contains a total of 119 individually addressable LEDs! The board is made by Pimoroni in the UK and is called a Scroll pHAT HD. The board comes with a female header, which normally you would solder onto the board to allow it to sit directly on top of your Pi Zero. However, we will adapt the board slightly so that we can conceal our Pi Zero and battery away out of sight and attach the board to an item of clothing as a badge.

We will look into the Python library, which Pimoroni supplies with the Scroll pHAT HD and try out a couple of different things that we can do with it.

We will finish our project off by installing a power-off switch to our Pi Zero, adding it into the official Pi Zero case and powering the whole setup from a portable battery pack.

You can find the Scroll pHAT HD over on Pimoroni's site at `https://shop.pimoroni.com /products/scroll-phat-hd`.

What we will cover

In this chapter, we will cover the following topics:

- What parts we will need to complete this project
- How to connect up the Scroll pHAT HD to our Pi Zero
- Installing the software to control our Scroll pHAT HD and writing our custom Python program for it

- Creating an off switch and an LED indicator for our Pi Zero, including writing the Python program for it
- Installing all of our electronics into our case and setting the Scroll pHAT HD up, so we can wear it as a badge

First off, let's look at what we will need for this project.

The bill of parts

We will make use of the following things in this project:

- A Pi Zero W
- A Scroll pHAT HD
- An official Pi Zero case
- A portable battery pack
- A push button switch
- A micro LED board
- Various cables to connect our parts
- Cable terminal block
- A sticky-backed badge pin
- Cable shrink wrap
- A hot glue gun
- Solder and a soldering iron

Putting the hardware together

First off, we need to connect up our hardware correctly so that we can begin to write our program to display our scrolling LED message! Let's first look at the Scroll pHAT HD.

Wiring up the Scroll pHAT HD

As we are not using the female header to place the Scroll pHAT HD directly on top of our Pi Zero, we need to first find out which pins from the GPIO header of the Pi Zero are required to run the Scroll pHAT HD. Fortunately, we can quite easily access this information from the Raspberry Pi Pinout website at `https://pinout.xyz/`.

Once you have opened the web page, click on the **Browse more HATS, pHATS and Add-ons** link in the top-right corner of the page, and find the link for **Scroll pHAT HD**. You can narrow your search by filtering by **Type=LED, Manufacturer=Pimoroni, Form factor=PHAT** from the filter menu on the left-hand side, as shown in the following screenshot:

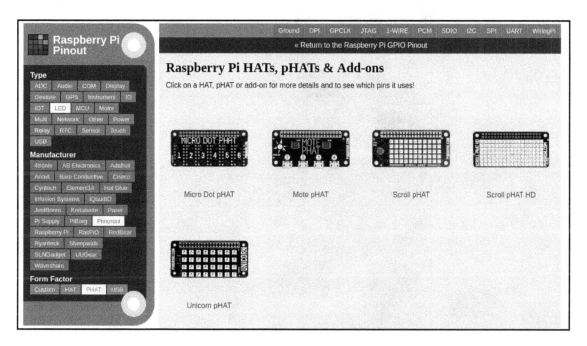

Once you have opened the Pinout page for the Scroll pHAT HD, you should see a detail of what pins the pHAT requires from the Pi to run, much like the following image. This tells us that the Scroll pHAT HD makes use of four pins: a ground pin, a 5V power(pin 2), and pins 3 and 5. We can use any of the ground pins indicated, so it would make sense to use pin 6 to keep everything close by.

The Scroll pHAT HD is a I2C device, and pins 3 and 5 (SDA and SCL) are the I2C data and clock pins respectively:

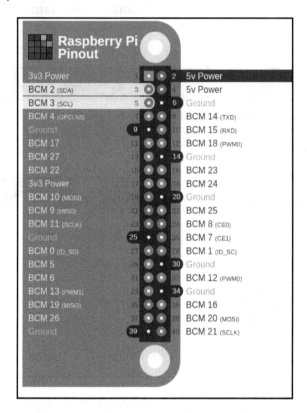

We need to prepare our cables for connecting to the Scroll pHAT HD. Cut about 30 cm of cable for each pin, and ensure you can identify which ends go to which pins on the Scroll pHAT HD! Ideally you will use four different colored wires for this part. Strip and tin one end of each cable, and then feed them through the back of your Scroll pHAT HD through the holes for pins 2, 3, 5, and 6 as shown next. Now, carefully solder each cable to the brass plate around the hole, and when you are happy that you have a good connection, clip any excess cable off with wire cutters.

You can now place some cable shrink wrap over the four cables, leaving about 4 cm free at the end. Heat the shrink wrap with a hair dryer until it shrinks around the cables, as shown in this picture:

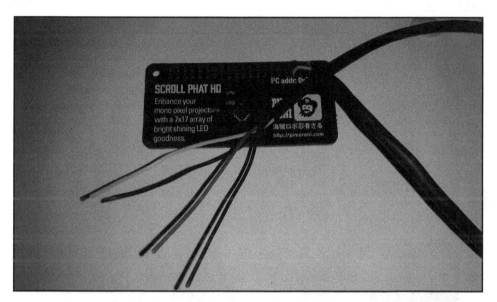

Wiring up the Pi

To enable us to easily connect and disconnect the Scroll pHAT HD to and from the Pi, we are going to make use of a small cable terminal block to connect the four cables from the Pi to the four cables on the Scroll pHAT HD. Cut your cable terminal block so that you have four pieces in a block.

We now need to cut enough cable so that when combined with the 30 cm of cable you attached to the Scroll pHAT HD earlier, we have enough cable to run from where you want to wear your scrolling badge to where you are going to conceal your Pi. If you are going to conceal your Pi in an inside packet, then another 30 cm should be more than adequate. Again, cut four wires to this length, matching the colors you used when connecting to the Scroll pHAT HD.

Strip and tin one end of each cable and feed them into the holes for pins 2, 3, 5, and 6 from the underside of the PI as shown here. When all the cables are in place solder each cable to the brass plate around the hole. When you are happy with your solder joints, trim any excess cable using wire cutters:

You can now shrink wrap this set of four cables in just the same way as you did with the four cables from the Scroll pHAT HD.

Attaching the Pi and the Scroll pHAT HD

Now that you have soldered your cables to both the Pi and the Scroll pHAT HD, we can connect them up and test that everything works as expected.

Strip the ends of all eight cables and tin them, so we get a sound connection. We can now feed each end into our block of four cable terminals, ensuring that the cables match either side of the terminal, as shown in this image. Tighten the screws in the terminal block and ensure that you have a sound connection by gently pulling on each cable to check it is secure:

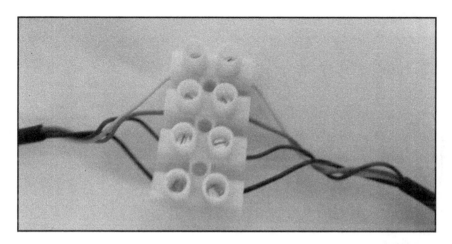

Installing and writing the software

Before we can begin testing, our Scroll pHAT HD and see what we can do with it, we need to install some software to our Pi.

First off, we need to ensure that the I2C interface on our Pi is enabled. Start your Pi up and connect to it via SSH. Now that you are connected, run the following command on your Pi to access the configuration tool:

```
sudo raspi-config
```

Now, select **5 Interfacing Options** using your cursors keys to highlight the menu option and then pressing *Enter*. In the Interfacing Options menu screen, highlight **P5 I2C,** and press *Enter* as shown in the following screenshot. In the next menu, select **Yes** and press *Enter,* and then press *Enter* to select **OK** to confirm the message that the ARM I2C interface is enabled. Press *Tab* twice to highlight **Finish** and press *Enter* to exit the `raspi-config` program. Now, type `sudo reboot now` to reboot your Pi:

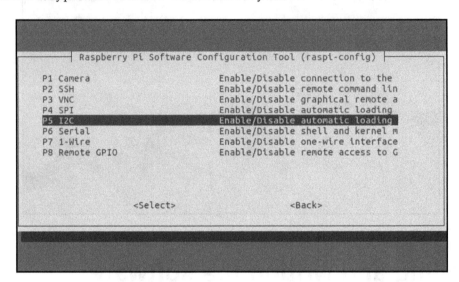

Once your Pi reboots, reconnect over SSH and type the following command to install the software we need to connect to our Scroll pHAT HD. This will also install all of the dependent software we need:

```
sudo apt-get install python3-scrollphathd -y
```

Once the software finishes downloading and installing ,we should first check that we can communicate to the Scroll pHAT HD on the correct I2C port.

Type the following command to query the I2C bus and see which channel the Scroll pHAT HD is connected to:

```
sudo i2cdetect -y 1
```

This should show you a result the same as in this image, letting us know that the Scroll pHAT HD is correctly connected to channel 74 on the I2C bus:

```
pi@wearablepi:~ $ sudo i2cdetect -y 1
     0  1  2  3  4  5  6  7  8  9  a  b  c  d  e  f
00:          -- -- -- -- -- -- -- -- -- -- -- -- --
10: -- -- -- -- -- -- -- -- -- -- -- -- -- -- -- --
20: -- -- -- -- -- -- -- -- -- -- -- -- -- -- -- --
30: -- -- -- -- -- -- -- -- -- -- -- -- -- -- -- --
40: -- -- -- -- -- -- -- -- -- -- -- -- -- -- -- --
50: -- -- -- -- -- -- -- -- -- -- -- -- -- -- -- --
60: -- -- -- -- -- -- -- -- -- -- -- -- -- -- -- --
70: -- -- -- -- 74 -- -- --
pi@wearablepi:~ $
```

Testing our Scoll pHAT HD

Now we know that we can communicate to our Scroll pHAT HD over the I2C bus, we can begin to write our first program to see it in all it's glory! Let's start with something basic just to check things are working as expected. As each LED on the Scroll pHAT HD is individually addressable, we can write some simple code to just light one LED. Connect to your Pi Zero via SSH and then let's move into our project directory by typing: cd ~/WearableTech/ and then create a new directory for this chapter by typing: mkdir Chapter2. Now move into that directory: cd Chapter2. Now, we will create a new Python file by typing nano basicLED.py; type the following code into the Nano text editor:

```
#!/usr/bin/python3

import scrollphathd as shd
from time import sleep

shd.set_pixel(4, 2, 0.5)
shd.show()
sleep(5)
```

Now, save and exit Nano by pressing *Ctrl + O*, followed by *Enter*, followed by *Ctrl + X*. We can now make our file executable by typing chmod +x ./basicLED.py , and then run it by typing ./basicLED.py.

All being well, we should see the pixel on the fifth column and the third row light up for 5 seconds (counting from the top left of the Scroll pHAT HD). Notice that when setting our pixel numbers in the `set_pixel` command, we start counting at zero, so the top left LED would be pixel (0, 0). The third number in the `set_pixel` command is brightness, with which we want to set the pixel; this can range form 0 (off) to 1 (full power). After making any change to the LEDs on the Scroll pHAT HD, we have to pass it the `show()` command before our changes will be displayed on the Scroll pHAT HD.

Great, so we now know that the Scroll pHAT HD works with our wiring and that we can control individual LEDs with a small piece of Python code, but what next?

Our scrolling badge program

Let's get straight on with writing the program for our scrolling badge. In this example, I am going to use my name, but the text that you have scrolling across your badge is really up to you. If your Pi Zero was online at the time you were wearing your badge, you could have this badge fetch the latest news from your favorite news feed and scroll that across, or even the weather where you are at the time.

To display text across our Scroll pHAT HD, we will make use of the `scroll()` function. Create a new file by typing `nano scrollBadge.py`. In your Nano text editor, type the following code.

 Take care when entering the lines inside the loop, as the number of spaces should match. I personally use four spaces for each level of indentation in my Python programs.

I have added comments into the code using the hash symbol to mark the start of each comment. They should explain what each step is doing:

```
#!/usr/bin/python3

import scrollphathd as shd #import our Scroll pHAT library
from time import sleep #import sleep from the time library

shd.clear() #clear any LEDs which are already lit
shd.show() #must call show after clear
shd.write_string("Hello, my name is Jon Witts!     ", brightness=0.25)
#The message to scroll with 5 spaces at the end
#the brightness sets the LEDs to 25%

while True: #We start a while loop which goes on forever
```

```
shd.show() #Show message on the LEDs
shd.scroll(1) #Scroll along the x-axis 1 pixel at a time
sleep(0.05) #Wait for 0.05 of a second before returning
             #to the start of the loop
```

Save your file by pressing *Ctrl + O,* followed by *Enter,* and then exit Nano by pressing *Ctrl + X.* Again, we now need to make our file executable by typing `chmod +x` `./scrollBadge.py;` and then run it by typing `./scrollBadge.py.`

All being well, you should see your message being scrolled across the LEDs on your Scroll pHAT HD. To stop your program from running, press *Ctrl + C* together. This program only really scratches the surface of what you can do with the Scroll pHAT HD. If you would like to know more then head over to the official documentation at `http://docs.pimoroni.com` `/scrollphathd/.`

So, we now have our message working on our Scroll pHAT HD, but we still have some work to do to be able to wear this as a badge!

Making our program start automatically

Needing to run our program over SSH is not any good if we want this to be a portable, wearable solution. We need to be able to just turn our set up on and have our message to start running automatically. To do this, we are going to create a systemd service definition, and activate it to run our Python program at a defined part of the Pi Zero's boot sequence.

 Be sure that you have tested your program, and it works as expected before doing this stage!

Creating our systemd service definition

Our systemd service definition is simply a text file saved into a particular location on our Pi Zero written in a certain format. We then activate the service definition by creating a **symlink** from the text file into the list of live services in another location on our Pi Zero.

So, let's start by creating the service definition. On your Pi Zero, type the following to open a new file in the Nano text editor:

```
sudo nano /lib/systemd/system/scrollBadge.service
```

Now, type the following text into Nano. Be sure to get the brackets and spacing correct:

```
[Unit]
Description=Scroll Badge Service
After=multi-user.target

[Service]
Type=idle
ExecStart=/home/pi/WearableTech/Chapter2/scrollBadge.py

[Install]
WantedBy=multi-user.target
```

> If you changed the names of any of the directories from earlier on, or saved your program to a different directory then you will need to update your `ExecStart` line to match the absolute path to your Python program.

Press *Ctrl + O* followed by *Enter* to save the file, and then *Ctrl + X* to exit Nano.

We now need to change the file permissions of the new service definition so that the system can read it at start up, and then reload the `systemd` configuration and enable our service file. Type the following three lines to carry out these steps:

```
sudo chmod 644 /lib/systemd/system/scrollBadge.service
sudo systemctl daemon-reload
sudo systemctl enable scrollBadge.service
```

If all went well with these three commands and no errors were shown, we can move on to test it. If you did get any errors, go back over each step and try to find what went wrong.

To test if our service definition is working, we need to restart the Pi Zero and check that our scrolling badge text runs automatically; do this by typing the following:

```
sudo reboot now
```

When your Pi Zero restarts, you should see that your text starts scrolling across your Scroll pHAT HD automatically. Reconnect to your Pi Zero over SSH and run the following command to double-check the status of your new service definition:

```
sudo systemctl status scrollBadge.service -l
```

All being well, you should see an output similar to the screenshot shown here:

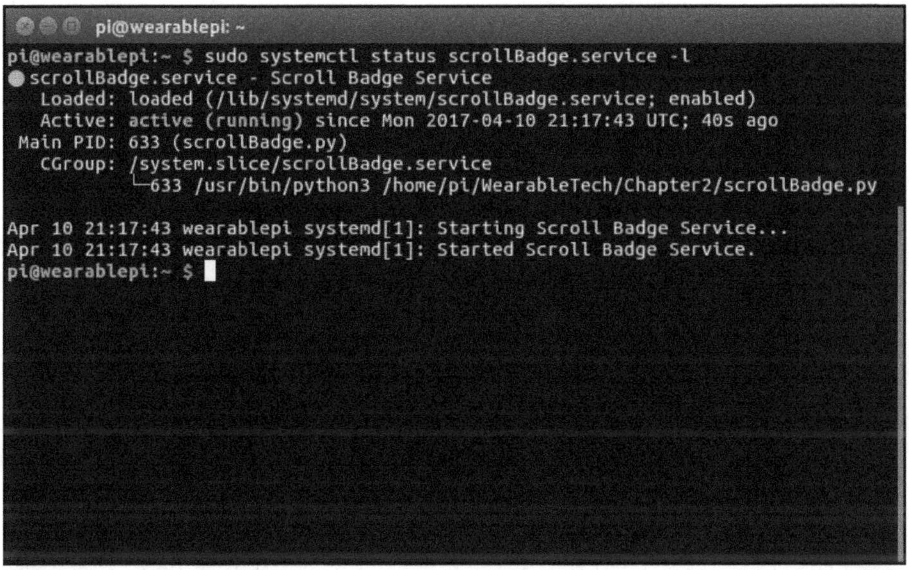

```
pi@wearablepi: ~
pi@wearablepi:~ $ sudo systemctl status scrollBadge.service -l
● scrollBadge.service - Scroll Badge Service
   Loaded: loaded (/lib/systemd/system/scrollBadge.service; enabled)
   Active: active (running) since Mon 2017-04-10 21:17:43 UTC; 40s ago
 Main PID: 633 (scrollBadge.py)
   CGroup: /system.slice/scrollBadge.service
           └─633 /usr/bin/python3 /home/pi/WearableTech/Chapter2/scrollBadge.py

Apr 10 21:17:43 wearablepi systemd[1]: Starting Scroll Badge Service...
Apr 10 21:17:43 wearablepi systemd[1]: Started Scroll Badge Service.
pi@wearablepi:~ $ █
```

Finalizing our hardware setup

Now that we have a working scrolling message on our Pi Zero, we need to look a little more at the hardware and how we will use this as a badge we can wear on our clothes. The first thing you will probably be thinking is that the two bare circuit boards of the Pi Zero, and the Scroll pHAT HD with all their cables between them do not make the best badge you have ever seen! But fear not, as this section of the project will get everything looking far neater and ready to go as a badge.

Wiring an off switch to our Pi Zero

We are going to solder two more pieces of hardware to our Pi Zero, which we will program to act as an off switch for our Pi Zero. This way, if we are using our Pi Zero out and about, we will not need a SSH connection to it to ensure we shut it down correctly.

I am going to use a push button switch from Kitronix for my button, but you could use any type push button. The one I have chosen is designed for eTextiles projects and comes presoldered to it's own little PCB; it is also very small as you can see in this picture (a micro SD card included for scale):

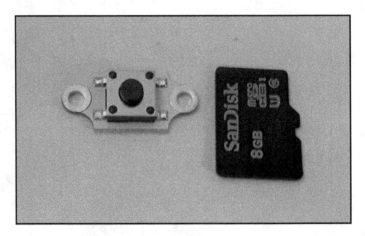

We now need to solder enough cable onto each side of the switch so that we can position it on the side of our case, about 5 cm should do the job. I have soldered 5 cm of red and black cable onto my switch, as shown in this picture here, and tinned the other ends of the cable, ready to attach to my Pi Zero:

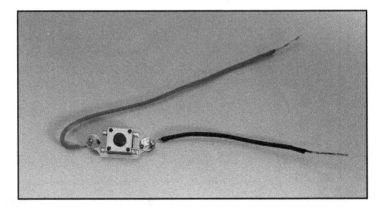

Push your cables through the back of the GPIO holes on your Pi Zero, as shown in this picture. I am making use of the bottom two GPIO holes here, GPIO 21 and a GND hole. It doesn't really matter which way around these go, but tradition dictates that the black cable should go to the GND hole and the red to the GPIO hole! Solder your cables into the holes on your Pi Zero and clip off any excess cable:

We are also going to attach a LED to the outside of our case, which will flash when we start the shutdown process. Again for this LED, I have chosen one from Kitronix, which is designed for eTextiles projects. The benefits here are the same as the switch; it comes on its own PCB (including the required resistor), and it is nice and small. This time, solder a slightly shorter length of cable, about 3 cm of red and black cable to the LED PCB, matching your red cable to the positive connection of the LED and your black cable to the negative connection, as shown in this picture. Trim any excess cable off with a pair of wire snips:

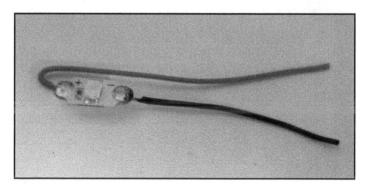

Now, strip and tin the other ends of the cable, and again feed them through the GPIO holes of your Pi Zero from the back into the GND and GPIO 16 holes. Be sure that the red cable goes to the GPIO 16 hole and the black cable to the GND hole, or our LED will not work! Have a look at the following picture:

Now, all four cables are through the Pi Zero in the correct place; turn it over and solder them in place. Once you are happy they are soldered correctly, remove any excess cable with wire snips.

Write our shutdown program

Now that we have connected our switch and LED, we need to write and test our program, which will gracefully shut down the Pi Zero if the button is pressed. We will use Python again for this, and then once we are sure the program works correctly, we will configure our Pi Zero to always run the program when we start our computer up.

Switch on your Pi Zero and connect to it over SSH. Now, move into our directory by typing `cd ~/WearableTech`. As we will use this shutdown switch for many of our projects, we will just create the Python file here as opposed to saving it in a subdirectory. Open Nano and create a new file called `shutdownPi.py` by typing `nano ./shutdownPi.py` and pressing *Enter* . In the empty text window which opens, type the following short Python program:

```python
#!/usr/bin/python3
from gpiozero import Button, LED
from signal import pause
from time import sleep
from os import system

button = Button(21, hold_time=3)
led = LED(16)

def shutdown_piZero():
    for i in range(3):
        led.on()
        sleep(0.5)
        led.off()
        sleep(0.5)
    system("sudo shutdown now -hP")

button.when_held = shutdown_piZero
pause()
```

Save the file by pressing *Ctrl* + *O*, followed by *Enter*, and then exit Nano by pressing *Ctrl* + *X*. We now need to make the file executable by typing this:

```
chmod +x ./shutdownPi.py
```

Now, we should test that it works before adding it as a startup service! Type `./shutdownPi.py` and try pressing and holding the button for one second (nothing should happen!). Press and hold the button for three seconds this time, and your LED should flash three times and then your Pi should begin it's shutdown process. If your Pi does not shutdown, then go back and check your Python program and the wiring between the button, LED, and Pi.

After your Pi has successfully shut down from your button press, turn it back on and log in again via SSH.

Making our shutdown program run automatically

Now that we have tested our shutdown program, we can make it start automatically. We will do this in the same way we did for the Scroll pHAT HD program, so I will not go into as much detail.

Create our service definition file:

```
sudo nano /lib/systemd/system/shutdownPi.service
```

Now type the definition into it:

```
[Unit]
Description=Shutdown Pi Service
After=multi-user.target

[Service]
Type=idle
ExecStart=/home/pi/WearableTech/shutdownPi.py

[Install]
WantedBy=multi-user.target
```

Save and exit Nano by typing *Ctrl + O,* followed by *Enter,* and then *Ctrl + X.* Now change the file permissions, reload the `systemd` daemon, and activate our service by typing this:

```
sudo chmod 644 /lib/systemd/system/shutdownPi.service
sudo systemctl daemon-reload
sudo systemctl enable shutdownPi.service
```

Now, we need to test this is working so reboot your Pi by typing `sudo reboot` , and then when your Pi Zero restarts and your message is scrolling, press and hold your newly soldered off switch for three seconds to check whether it shuts down correctly and your LED flashes as expected.

Putting it all together

So, now we have all of our hardware connected up and tested and we also have our software written and tested, however we still need to carry out a few more steps to complete our project. We need to install our Pi Zero in its case and attach our switch and LED to the outside of the case, and we also need to enable us to wear the Scroll pHAT HD as a badge.

Installing the Pi Zero into its case

We are going to make use of the official Pi Zero case in this project. It has a really easy access to the GPIO pin holes on the board and is nice and compact too. If you have a different case, then you should be able to adapt these steps to use that case instead.

To start with, you will want to disconnect the cables running from the Pi to the Scroll pHAT HD from the terminal block. I should also note that it would be best to carry these steps out with your Pi switched off!

You now need to carefully feed the cables and the through the GPIO access at the back of the case, and also feed the off switch and LED through this hole as shown in this picture. You should now be able to push the Pi zero back into place in the case until it clips in. It can be seen in the following picture:

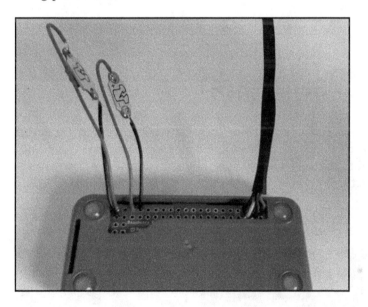

Take the off switch, and line it up to the side of the case so the cables are neatly lined up across the back of the case. You can put a few twists in the cables so that they stay close to each other. Once you are happy with the placement of your switch, apply a little hot glue to the case and firmly press the switch into it. Be careful that you do not get any glue going over the side of the case, as this will make it harder to put the top on later. Now, do the same with your LED and glue to your case in a similar fashion. Be careful to ensure that the button and LED do not touch each other on your case.

You can now attach the lid to your case, and you should have something looking like this picture:

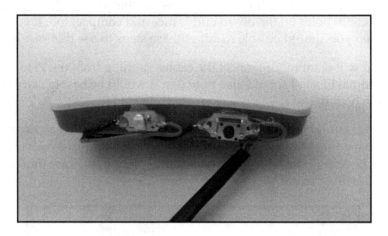

Making our Scroll pHAT HD badge

We now need to carry out a final step so that we can wear our Scroll pHAT HD as a badge; we need to make it into a badge! To do this, I am using a badge pin, which you should be able to get from any hobby or craft shop. The ones I have came with double-sided tape to attach them to your badge, so I made use of this to attach it to my Scroll pHAT HD as shown in this picture:

We can now wear our Scroll pHAT HD badge with pride! I have pinned my badge to my jacket and can then feed the cable inside my jacket by either making a small hole behind the badge and feeding the cables through, or finding another route to get the cables to the pocket where I am going to conceal my Pi Zero. Once you have the cables feed through, reconnect the cables from the Scroll pHAT HD to the Pi Zero using the terminal block, and neaten any extra cables up by pulling them into your pocket.

We will, of course, need a portable power source to run our Pi Zero and Scroll pHAT HD; for this, I am using a simple portable battery pack, which you can use for charging your phone when you are out and about.

Plug your battery pack into your Pi Zero, and your Scroll pHAT HD badge should begin scrolling you message across it's screen in a few minutes. To switch off your badge, just hold the off switch on the side of your Raspberry Pi Zero case down for three seconds! The output can be seen in the following picture:

Summary

In this project, we have looked at an add-on piece of hardware for the Raspberry Pi and the Scroll pHAT HD; we also saw how we can adapt this to work in our projects. You also learned about sources of information about how we need to wire these add-ons to our Raspberry Pi computers if we are not using the standard **hat** method; this will come in useful in future projects too!

We then looked at how we can control the Scroll pHAT HD add-on board with some simple Python code. There is plenty of scope here for personalizing this project here, and we now know where to find the online documentation to learn what else this board can do.

Another important step covered was to make Python programs we write start automatically when we power up our Pi Zero. We did this twice just in this project, and this is something we will need to do for most of the remaining projects in the book.

Finally, you learned how to connect a switch to the outside of our Raspberry Pi case, so we have a way to safely switch off our Pi without potentially damaging our SD card and our programs on it.

3
Sewable LEDs in Clothing

In this project, we will use sewable LEDs and conductive threads to transform the item of clothing into a sparkling LED piece of wearable tech, controlled with our Pi Zero hidden in the clothing. We will incorporate Pi Zero and a battery into a hidden pocket in the garment and connect our sewable LEDs to the Pi's GPIO pins so that we can write Python code to control the order and timings of the LEDs.

If you are using the same Pi Zero for this project as you did for the previous project, desolder the four cables, which lead from Pi Zero to the Scroll pHAT HD, but leave your off switch and LED in place; you may need to detach these from the case first. To deactivate the software running automatically, connect to your Pi Zero over SSH and issue the following command:

```
sudo systemctl disable scrollBadge.service
```

Once this command completes, you can shutdown your Pi Zero by pressing your off switch for three seconds. Now, let's look at what we are going to cover in this chapter.

What We Will Cover

In this chapter, we will cover the following topics:

- What we will need to complete this project
- How we will modify our item of clothing
- Writing a Python program to control electronics in our modified garment
- Making our program run automatically

Let's jump straight in and look at what parts we will need to complete this project.

The bill of parts

We will make use of the following things in this project:

- A Pi Zero W
- An official Pi Zero case
- A portable battery pack
- An item of clothing to modify, for example, a top or t-shirt
- 10 sewable LEDs
- Conductive threads
- Some fabric the same color as the clothing
- Threads as the same color as the clothing
- A sewing needle
- Pins
- Six metal poppers
- Some black and yellow colored cable
- Solders and soldering iron

Modifying our item of clothing

So let's take a look at what we need to do to modify our item of clothing ready to accommodate our Pi Zero, a battery pack, and sewable LEDs. We will start by looking at creating our hidden pocket for Pi Zero and the batteries, followed by how we will sew our LEDs into the top and design our sewable circuit. We will then solve the problem of connecting our conductive thread back to the GPIO holes on our Pi Zero.

Our hidden pocket

You will need a piece of fabric that is large enough to house your Pi Zero case and battery pack alongside each other with enough spare to hem the pocket all the way round. If you have access to a sewing machine, then this section of the project will be much quicker, otherwise you will need to do the stitching by hand.

The piece of fabric I am using is 18 x 22 cm allowing for a 1 cm hem all around. Fold and pin the 1 cm hem, and then either stitch it by hand or run it through a sewing machine to secure your hem. When you have finished, remove the pins.

You need to then turn your garment inside out and decide where you are going to position your hidden pocket. As I am using a t-shirt for my garment, I am going to position my pocket just inside at the bottom side of the garment, wrapping around the front and back so that it sits across the wearer's hip. Pin your pocket in place, and then stitch it along the bottom, left, and right sides, leaving the top open. Make sure that you stitch this nice and firmly as it has to hold the weight of your battery pack. The picture here shows you my pocket after being stitched in place. When you have finished, this you can remove the pins, and turn your garment the correct way round again:

Adding our sewable LEDs

We are now going to plan our circuit for our sewable LEDs and add them to the garment. I am going to run a line of 10 LEDs around the bottom of my top. These will be wired up in pairs so that we can control a pair of LEDs at any one time with our Pi Zero. You can position your LEDs howsoever you want, but it is important that the circuits of conductive thread do not cross or touch one another.

Turn your garment inside out again and mark with a washable pen where you want your LEDs to be sewn. As the fabric for my garment is quite light, I am going to just stitch them inside and let the LED shine through the material. However, if your material is heavier than you expected, then you will have to put a small cut where each LED will be, and then button hole the cut so that the LED can push through. Start with the LED furthest from your hidden pocket. Once you have your LED in position, take a length of your conductive thread and over sew the negative hole of your LED to your garment, trying to keep your stitches as small and as neat as possible, to minimize how much they can be seen from the front of the garment.

You now need to stitch small running stitches from the first LED to the second; ensure that you use the same piece of conductive thread and do not cut it! When you get to the position of your LED, again over sew the negative hole of your LED ensuring that it is face down so that the LED shows through the fabric. As I am stitching my LEDs quite close to the hem of my t-shirt, I have made use of the hem to run the conductive thread in when connecting the negative holes of the LEDs, as shown in the image here:

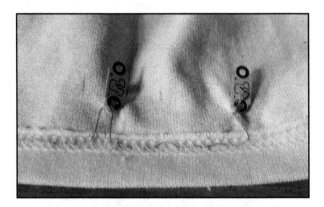

Continue on connecting each negative point of your LEDs to each other with a single length of conductive thread. Your final LED will be the one closest to your hidden pocket, continue with a running stitch until you are on your hidden pocket. Now, take the male half of one of your metal poppers and over sew this in place through one of the holes. You can now cut the length of conductive thread, as we have completed our common ground circuit for all the LEDs.

When cutting the conductive thread, be sure to leave a very short end. If two pieces of the thread were to touch when we were powering the LEDs, we could cause a short circuit. You can use a bit of clear nail varnish to seal the ends of the thread.

Now, stitch the three remaining holes with standard thread, as shown in this picture:

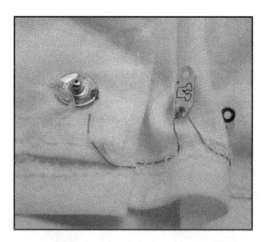

We now need to sew our positive connections to our garment. Start with a new length of conductive thread, and attach the LED second closest to your hidden pocket. Again over-sew it it to the fabric, trying to ensure that your stitches are as small as possible, so they are not very visible from the front of the garment. Now that you have secured the first LED, sew a small running stitch to the positive connection on the LED closest to the hidden pocket. After securing this LED, stitch a running stitch so that it stops alongside the popper you previously secured to your pocket. And this time, attach a female half of a metal popper in the same way as before, as shown in this picture:

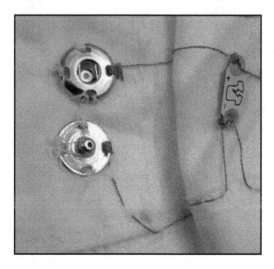

Secure your remaining eight LEDs in the same fashion: working in pairs and away from the pocket so that you are left with one male metal popper and five female metal poppers in a line on your hidden pocket. Ensure that the six different conductive threads do not cross at any point, the six poppers do not touch, and that you have the positive and negative connections the right way round! The picture here shows you the completed circuit stitched into the t-shirt, terminating at the poppers on the pocket:

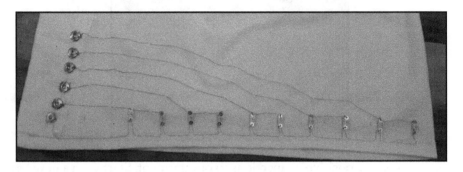

Connecting our Pi Zero

Now that we have our electrical circuit, we need to find a way to attach our Pi Zero to each pair of LEDs and the common ground we have sewn into our garment. We are going to make use of the poppers we stitched onto our hidden pocket for this. You have probably noticed that the only piece of conductive thread, which we attached the male popper to, was the common ground thread for our LEDs. This is so that when we construct our method of attaching the Pi Zero GPIO pins to the conductive thread, it will be impossible to connect the positive and negative threads the wrong way round! Another reason for using the poppers to attach our Pi Zero to the conductive thread is because the LEDs and thread I am using are both rated as OK for hand washing, your Pi Zero is not!

Take your remaining female popper and solder a length of black cable to it, about two and a half times the height of your hidden pocket should do the job. You can feed the cable through one of the holes in the popper as shown in the picture to ensure you get a good connection. For the five remaining male poppers, solder the same length of yellow cable to each popper. The picture here shows two of my soldered poppers:

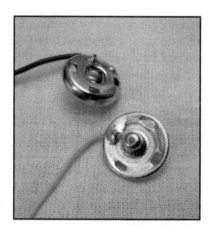

Now, connect all of your poppers to the other parts on your garment and carefully bend all the cables so that they all run in the same direction: up toward the top of your hidden pocket. Trim all the cable to the same length, and then mark the top and bottom of each yellow cable with a permanent marker so that you know which cable is attached to which pair of LEDs. I am marking the bottom yellow cable as number 1 and the top as number 5. We can now cut a length of heat shrink and cover the loose lengths of cable, leaving about 4 cm free to strip, tin, and solder onto your Pi. You can now heat the heat shrink with a hair dryer to shrink it around your cables:

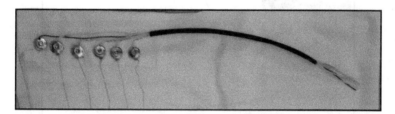

We are now going to stitch together a small piece of fabric to attach the poppers to. We want to end up with a piece of fabric that is large enough to sew all six poppers to without them touching each other, and also leave enough space to allow us to stitch the uncovered cables down to. This will be used to detach Pi Zero from our garment when we need to wash it; or just remove our Pi Zero for another project. To strengthen up the fabric, I am doubling it over and hemming a long and short side of the fabric to make a pocket. This can then be turned inside out, and the remaining short side can be stitched over.

You now need to position these poppers onto your piece of fabric so that they are aligned with the poppers you have sewn into your garment. Once you are happy with their placement, stitch them to the piece of fabric using standard thread, ensuring that they are really firmly attached. If you like, you can also put a few stitches over each cable to ensure they stay in place too.

Using a fine permanent marker, number both the ends of the 5 yellow cables 1 through 5 so that you can identify each cable. Now, push all six cables through about 12 cm of shrink wrap and apply some heat from a hair dryer until it shrinks around your cables. You now need to strip and tin the ends of the six cables so that they are ready to solder onto your Pi Zero. Insert the black cable in the ground hole below GPIO 11 on your Pi Zero, and then insert the 5 yellow cables sequentially, 1 through 5, into the GPIO holes 11, 9, 10, 7 and 8, as shown in this diagram, again from the rear of Pi Zero. When you are happy and all the cables are in the correct place, solder them to your Pi Zero and clip off any extra length from the front of the Pi Zero with wire snips:

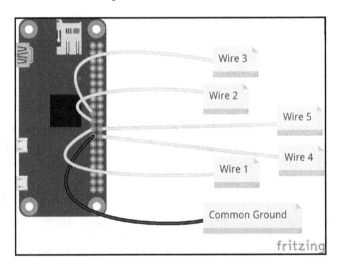

You should now be able to connect your Pi Zero to your LEDs by pressing all six poppers together. To ensure that the wearer's body does not cause a short circuit with the conductive thread on the inside of the garment, you may want to take another piece of fabric, and stitch it over all of the conductive thread lines. I would recommend that you do this after you have tested all your LEDs with the program in the next section. We have now carried out all the modifications needed for our garment, so let's move onto writing our Python program to control our LEDs.

Writing our Python program

To start with, we will write a simple, short piece of Python just to check that all ten of our LEDs are working, and we know which GPIO pin controls which pair of LEDs. Power on your Pi Zero and connect to it via SSH.

Testing our LEDs

To check that our LEDs are all correctly wired up and that we can control them using Python, we will write this short program to test them.

First, move into our project directory by typing this:

> **cd ~/WearableTech/**

Now, make a new directory for this chapter by typing this:

> **mkdir Chapter3**

Now, move into our new directory:

> **cd Chapter3**

Next, we create our test program by typing this:

> **nano testLED.py**

Then, we enter the following code into Nano:

```
#!/usr/bin/python3

from gpiozero import LED
from time import sleep

pair1 = LED(11)
pair2 = LED(9)
pair3 = LED(10)
pair4 = LED(7)
pair5 = LED(8)

for i in range(4):
    pair1.on()
    sleep(2)
    pair1.off()
    pair2.on()
    sleep(2)
```

```
        pair2.off()
        pair3.on()
        sleep(2)
        pair3.off()
        pair4.on()
        sleep(2)
        pair4.off()
        pair5.on()
        sleep(2)
        pair5.off()
```

Press *Ctrl + O* followed by *Enter* to save the file, and then *Ctrl + X* to exit Nano. We can then run our file by typing this:

```
python3 ./testLED.py
```

All being well, we should see each pair of LEDs light up for two seconds in turn, and then the next pair; and the whole loop should repeat four times.

Our final LED program

We will now write our Python program, which will control our LEDs in our t-shirt. This will be the program that we configure to run automatically when we power up our Pi Zero. So let's begin:

Create a new file by typing this:

```
nano tShirtLED.py
```

Now, type the following Python program into Nano:

```
#!/usr/bin/python3

from gpiozero import LEDBoard
from time import sleep
from random import randint

leds = LEDBoard(11, 9, 10, 7, 8)

while True:
    for i in range(5):
        wait = randint(5,10)/10
        leds.on()
        sleep(wait)
        leds.off()
        sleep(wait)
```

```
for i in range(5):
    wait = randint(5,10)/10
    leds.value = (1, 0, 1, 0, 1)
    sleep(wait)
    leds.value = (0, 1, 0, 1, 0)
    sleep(wait)
for i in range(5):
    wait = randint(1,5)/10
    leds.value = (1, 0, 0, 0, 0)
    sleep(wait)
    leds.value = (1, 1, 0, 0, 0)
    sleep(wait)
    leds.value = (1, 1, 1, 0, 0)
    sleep(wait)
    leds.value = (1, 1, 1, 1, 0)
    sleep(wait)
    leds.value = (1, 1, 1, 1, 1)
    sleep(wait)
    leds.value = (1, 1, 1, 1, 0)
    sleep(wait)
    leds.value = (1, 1, 1, 0, 0)
    sleep(wait)
    leds.value = (1, 1, 0, 0, 0)
    sleep(wait)
    leds.value = (1, 0, 0, 0, 0)
    sleep(wait)
```

Now, save your file by pressing *Ctrl + O* followed by *Enter*, then exit Nano by pressing *Ctrl + X*. Test that your program is working correctly by typing this:

```
python3 ./tShirtLED.py
```

If there are any errors displayed, go back and check your program in Nano. Once your program has gone through the three different display patterns, press *Ctrl + C* to stop the program from running.

We have introduced a number of new things in this program. Firstly, we imported a new GPIOZero library item called LEDBoard. LEDBoard lets us define a list of GPIO pins, which have LEDs attached to them and perform actions on our list of LEDs rather than having to operate them all one at a time. It also lets us pass a value to the LEDBoard object, which indicates whether to turn the individual members of the board on or off. We also imported randint from the random library. randint allows us to get a random integer in our program, and we can also pass it a start and end value from which the random integer should be taken. We then define three different loop patterns and set each of them inside a for loop, which repeats five times.

Making our program start automatically

We now need to make our `tShirtLED.py` program run automatically when we switch our Pi Zero on. We are going to do this in the same way we did in the previous chapters:

First, we must make the Python program we just wrote executable:

```
chmod +x ./tShirtLED.py
```

Now, we will create our service definition file by typing this:

```
sudo nano /lib/systemd/system/tShirtLED.service
```

Now, type the definition into it:

```
[Unit]
Description=tShirt LED Service
After=multi-user.target

[Service]
Type=idle
ExecStart=/home/pi/WearableTech/Chapter3/tShirtLED.py

[Install]
WantedBy=multi-user.target
```

Save and exit Nano by typing *Ctrl + O* followed by *Enter*, and then *Ctrl + X*. Now, change the file permissions, reload the `systemd` daemon, and activate our service by typing this:

```
sudo chmod 644 /lib/systemd/system/tShirtLED.service
sudo systemctl daemon-reload
sudo systemctl enable tShirtLED.service
```

Now, we need to test whether this is working, so reboot your Pi by typing `sudo reboot`, and then when your Pi Zero restarts, you should see that your LED pattern starts to display automatically. Once you are happy that it is all working correctly, press and hold your power-off button for three seconds to shut your Pi Zero down.

You can now turn your garment the right way round and install Pi Zero and battery pack into your hidden pocket. As soon as you plug your battery pack into Pi Zero, your LEDs will start to display their patterns; and you can safely turn it all off using your power-off button we installed in Chapter 2, *Scrolling LED Badge*:

Summary

In this chapter, we looked at making use of stitchable electronics and how we could combine them with our Pi Zero. We made our first stitchable circuit and found a way that we could connect our Pi Zero to this circuit and control the electronic devices using the GPIO Zero Python library. We will expand upon this skill in a future chapter to make a more complete wearable tech t-shirt design.

4
A Motion-Reactive LED Cap

We will make use of a Pimoroni Blinkt LED strip, an Adafruit Triple-Axis Accelerometer, and Pi Zero to create a hat with a super-bright strip of eight RGB LEDs across the front, which will change their colors and display based upon the direction you move in.

If you are using the same Pi Zero for this project as you did for the previous project, desolder the six cables, which lead from the Pi Zero to the poppers, but leave your off switch and LED in place, as you may need to detach these from the case first. To deactivate the software running automatically, connect to your Pi Zero over SSH and issue the following command:

```
sudo systemctl disable tShirtLED.service
```

Once the command completes, you can shut down your Pi Zero by pressing your off switch for three seconds. Now, let's look at what we are going to cover in this chapter.

What we will cover

In this chapter, we will cover the following topics:

- What we will need to complete this project
- Connecting our hardware to the Pi Zero
- Modifying our cap
- Writing our program
- Making our program run automatically

Let's jump straight in and look at what parts we will need to complete this project.

The bill of parts

We will make use of the following things in this project:

- A Pi Zero W
- An official Pi Zero case
- A portable battery pack and a long USB to micro USB cable
- An Adafruit ADXL345 Triple-Axis Accelerometer
- A Pimoroni Blinkt LED strip
- A break away header strip
- Cable heat shrink
- A baseball cap
- Some thread
- A sewing needle
- Some self-adhesive Velcro
- Some black, red, blue, and yellow colored cables
- Solders and soldering iron
- A hot glue gun

Connecting our hardware

Let's begin this project by getting all the hardware set up and connected. Once connect each piece of hardware, we will do a quick test to check whether it is working as expected before moving on.

Let's start with the accelerometer.

Connecting our accelerometer

To communicate with our accelerometer, we need to connect four of the points on the board to four of the GPIO points on Pi Zero. The ADXL345 board uses I2C, so we will be using the same connections as we did with the Scroll pHAT HD, except we will be using a 3.3V power instead of a 5V power this time. This diagram shows us how we need to connect the ADXL345 to our Pi Zero:

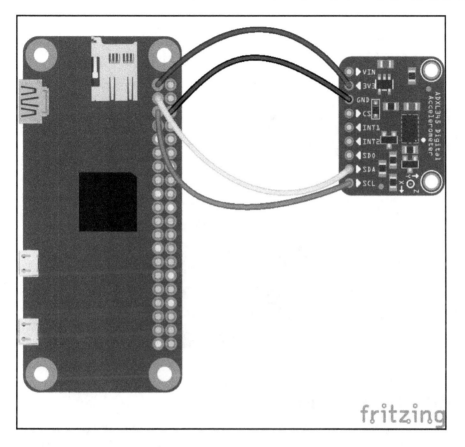

As the ADXL345 is such a tiny board, we will be locating it in the lid of our Pi Zero case. Strip and tin each end of a black, red, yellow, and blue wire so that they are about 5 cm long. This time we are going to solder them to the front of the board, as this wiring will all remain inside our case. Solder the four cables to your Pi Zero and ADXL345 as shown in the preceding diagram. Trim back any excess cable from both the Pi and ADXL345. Give the ADXL345 a couple of turns just to twist the four wires together to keep them neat in your case.

You can now install the ADXL345 into the white lid of your Pi Zero case. Apply a little hot glue to the center of the lid and firmly press the underside of the ADXL345 into the glue. You can see my ADXL345 wired up and glued into my case in this picture:

Testing our accelerometer

We are now ready to test our ADXL345 to check that we can read the data from it into Python. Power up your Pi Zero and connect to it over SSH. Move into your project directory by typing cd WearableTech, and then make a new directory for this chapter by typing mkdir Chapter4 ; and now move into that new directory by typing cd Chapter4.

Pimoroni has provided a Python library for the Adafruit ADXL345 accelerometer, which is available on their GitHub page at https://github.com/pimoroni/adxl345-python; however, this library is written for Python 2, and we are using Python 3. I have cloned this repository in GitHub and adjusted it so that it works for Python 3. We will make use of this library to access and test our ADXL345.

Before we access the ADXL345 over Python, we should check that it is being correctly detected on the I2C bus. If you didn't follow the project in Chapter 2, *Scrolling LED Badge*, or you are carrying this project out on a new SD card, and then you will need to enable the I2C bus on your Pi Zero. Head over to Chapter 2, *Scrolling LED Badge*, and follow the steps there if you need to.

Now, we have the I2C bus enabled, issue the following command to test, which address our ADXL345 I2C device is detected on, `sudo i2cdetect -y 1`. You should see something like this:

```
 Terminal  File  Edit  View  Search  Terminal  Help
pi@wearablepi:~/WearableTech/Chapter4 $ sudo i2cdetect -y 1
     0  1  2  3  4  5  6  7  8  9  a  b  c  d  e  f
00:          -- -- -- -- -- -- -- -- -- -- -- --
10: -- -- -- -- -- -- -- -- -- -- -- -- -- -- -- --
20: -- -- -- -- -- -- -- -- -- -- -- -- -- -- -- --
30: -- -- -- -- -- -- -- -- -- -- -- -- -- -- -- --
40: -- -- -- -- -- -- -- -- -- -- -- -- -- -- -- --
50: -- -- -- 53 -- -- -- -- -- -- -- -- -- -- -- --
60: -- -- -- -- -- -- -- -- -- -- -- -- -- -- -- --
70: -- -- -- -- -- -- -- --
pi@wearablepi:~/WearableTech/Chapter4 $ 
```

This is telling us that we have a device on address 53 of the I2C bus, which is good because this is the address that we are expecting ADXL345 to be present on!

Now, we are going to clone the modified GitHub repository and check whether we can get readings from our ADXL345 into Python. We need to install Git to carry these steps out, but before installing the new software, it is best to update and upgrade what we have already. Issue this command to update and upgrade the software on your Pi Zero:

```
sudo apt-get update && sudo apt-get upgrade -y
```

When this completes, we can now install Git. Git is a software version control system, and GitHub is a web-based Git system, which many developers around the world use for sharing and collaborating on software projects together. Issue the following command to install Git:

```
sudo apt-get install git -y
```

Once the install process completes, we can now copy or clone the GitHub repository from my GitHub account with the Python library we need to communicate with ADXL345 in Python 3. Type the following command to clone the ADXL345 libraries into the current directory:

```
git clone https://github.com/jonwitts/adxl345-python.git
```

If you type `ls -l`, you will notice that you now have a new directory called `adxl345-python`; move into this directory by typing `cd adxl345-python`, and then list the contents of this directory by typing `ls -l`. You will see something similar to this picture:

```
pi@wearablepi: ~/WearableTech/Chapter4/adxl345-python
pi@wearablepi:~/WearableTech/Chapter4/adxl345-python $ ls -l
total 16
-rw-r--r-- 1 pi pi 3181 Apr 30 10:31 adxl345.py
-rw-r--r-- 1 pi pi  634 Apr 30 10:31 example.py
-rw-r--r-- 1 pi pi 1504 Apr 30 10:31 LICENSE.txt
-rw-r--r-- 1 pi pi  893 Apr 30 10:31 README.md
pi@wearablepi:~/WearableTech/Chapter4/adxl345-python $
```

The file we are interested in here is `example.py`. Run it by typing this:

```
python3 ./example.py
```

All being well, you should see something like this picture being output to your SSH connection:

```
pi@wearablepi:~/WearableTech/Chapter4/adxl345-python
    y = -0.040G
    z = -0.916G
---------------------------------------------
ADXL345 on address 0x53:
    x = -0.028G
    y = -0.044G
    z = -0.916G
---------------------------------------------
ADXL345 on address 0x53:
    x = -0.040G
    y = -0.052G
    z = -0.912G
---------------------------------------------
ADXL345 on address 0x53:
    x = -0.028G
    y = -0.036G
    z = -0.912G
---------------------------------------------
ADXL345 on address 0x53:
    x = -0.032G
    y = -0.048G
    z = -0.900G
---------------------------------------------
```

If you rotate your Pi Zero through its three rotational axis, you should see these values changing. We are reading the force on ADXL345 in a measurement of g, the gravitational pull from the earth's gravity. As we rotate and move ADXL345 through each of its axis, we can see that reading of force change. Stop the example.py program from running by pressing *Ctrl* + *C* on your keyboard.

Once we have stopped the ADXL345 example from running, we can turn off our Pi Zero by holding your power-off switch in for three seconds. Leave it for a few seconds after the light finishes flashing to allow the Pi Zero to shut down completely, and then remove the power from your Pi Zero.

Next, we are going to look at connecting Blinkt to our Pi Zero.

Connecting our Blinkt

The wiring for Blinkt is going to be a little bit trickier, as it does not come with a header to be soldered on, it is already soldered for us. This means we will need to solder directly to some break away header strip so that we can connect and disconnect our Pi Zero from Blinkt safely. First of all, we need to find out which pins need connecting to what on Pi Zero. Once again, we can make use of the Raspberry Pi *Pinout* website to tell us this. Head over to `https://pinout.xyz/pinout/blinkt`, and you will see that Blinkt requires four connections to our Pi Zero, a 5V power, a ground, and GPIO pins—23 and 24.

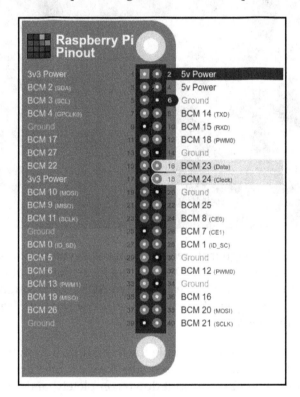

Take a strip of the break away header and snap off a length of 10 pins. You now need to cut, strip, and tin one end of 20 cm length of red, black, yellow, and blue cables. Strip and twist the other ends so that there are no stray wires. You now need to take your cables and twist them around the header pins as shown here. Be sure to check carefully that there are no stray wires that could short across to another pin. The red cable should go around the first pin, the black around the third pin, the blue around the eighth pin, and the yellow around the ninth one. Once you have twisted the cables around the pins, and you are happy that there are no stray cables, you need to apply some solder to each pin to secure the cables in place. Ensure that you work quickly and accurately here as the plastic of break away headers has a habit of melting if you apply too much heat to it! Soldering can be seen in the following picture:

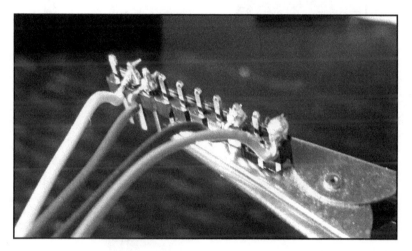

To finish this connection cable off, twist your four cables together and shrink wrap, leaving about 2-3 cm of cables out of the other end, ready to solder to your Pi Zero.

To connect these cables up to your Pi Zero, take the tinned tips and push them through the back of your Pi Zero so that the connecting cable that we just made feeds through the GPIO access hole in the base of the case. Solder each cable to your Pi Zero, as indicated in the diagram here, and then clip off any excess cable length before carefully closing up your case:

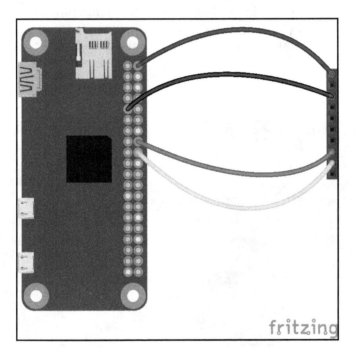

Now that we have soldered on our connecting cable, we can connect it up to our Blinkt LED strip and test that it works.

Testing Blinkt

First, connect your cable headers into Blinkt. The pin with the red cable attached needs to connect to the hole nearest Pimoroni Pirate, which is in the top row with the curved edges of the Blinkt at the top. You can see my cable connected in this picture:

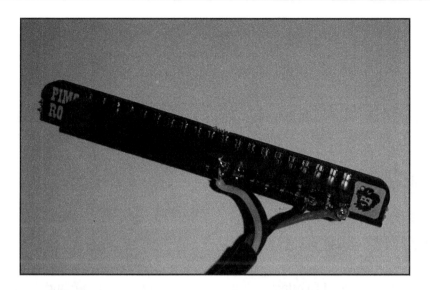

Before we can test our Blinkt, we need to download some software to our Pi Zero. Power up your Pi Zero and connect to it over SSH. As per the documentation over on Pimoroni's site at https://learn.pimoroni.com/tutorial/sandyj/getting-started-with-blinkt, we will install the Blinkt Python library by issuing the following command:

```
curl https://get.pimoroni.com/blinkt | bash
```

Press *Y* and *Enter* to confirm that we want to continue and then wait for a bit while the script gets everything ready. When you are asked if you would like to perform a full install, press *Y* and *Enter* to continue. The installer will then install Blinkt Python libraries as well as example programs and the dependencies for these programs. When this completes, you should be greeted with a message saying:

```
Downloading examples and documentation...
 Resources for your Blinkt! were copied to
 /home/pi/Pimoroni/blinkt
 All done. Enjoy your Blinkt!!
```

So, let's move into the examples inside the resources directory, which we have just installed. Type this:

```
cd ~/Pimoroni/blinkt/examples
```

If you type `ls`, you will see all of the different examples available here. To just test that our Blinkt is working correctly, type this:

```
python3 ./rainbow.py
```

All being well, your Blinkt should light up and scroll a rainbow of colors across it's eight LEDs. When you have had enough of staring at the beautiful lights, press *Ctrl* and *C* to quit the `rainbow.py` program from running. You can then shut down your Pi Zero by pressing and holding your power-off button for three seconds.

Next, we will look at modifying our hat and installing our hardware into it.

Modifying our cap

To install our hardware into our baseball cap, we will need to make a few minor modifications! We will need to attach our Blinkt to the front of the cap and feed it to the attaching cable, which is soldered to Pi Zero through the hat; and attach the Pi Zero to the back of the cap. We will use a long USB to Micro USB cable so that we can keep the battery in our pocket and run the cable up to our cap to power Pi Zero.

We need to make a small hole in the cap to feed the cable with the pins soldered onto the end of it through our cap. We are going to end up with the strip of eight LEDs sitting on the peak of the cap, central aligned. As the cable connects to the left hand side of the LED strip (as you look at it), we will make our cut into the cap on the your right hand side of the cap (if you had it on your head!). Position the Blinkt strip at the peak of the hat so that it is centrally aligned, and then mark with a pencil where you need the cable to come through the hat. Cut a hole about 1-1.5 cm in the hat where you marked it, and then either put some stitches around it to stop the hole from fraying, or iron some hem webbing to the back of the hole. You can now carefully feed your cable through the hole.

Attach your Blinkt strip to your cable, and check whether it is still aligned centrally on the peak. The cap I am using has a band around the inside of the cap, which I will make use of to run the cable round the cap to where we install Pi Zero. I have folded this band down, and then marked where the cable meets the band as it enters the hat. Remove your Blinkt strip from the cable, turn your cap over, and stitch a few stitches over the cable to secure to the inner band at the correct point.

Now that your cable is held in the right place, turn your hat over and stitch over the pins of the attachment cable a few times to hold it back to the cap in the correct position. As you do this, check whether it is being secured in the correct place by attaching your Blinkt strip and adjusting it as necessary. Once you are happy that the pins are secured in the correct place to attach your Blinkt strip centrally, turn your cap over and continue stitching the cable into the inside of the head band. Keep going around the head band until the Pi Zero can be fed out of the hole at the back of the cap.

Now, take a piece of self-adhesive Velcro, and stick it to the back of the Pi Zero case. Take the other half of the Velcro and sew it onto the back of the cap so that Pi Zero can be attached to the back of your cap with the power socket facing down.

You can now attach the Blinkt strip to the front of your cap and try it on for size! Here is a picture of the front and back of my modified cap:

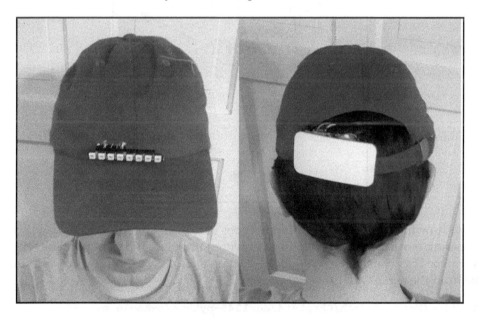

Writing our program

Now that we have set up, tested, and installed all of the hardware into our cap, we can begin writing the program for it. Connect your Pi Zero to a power source, and then connect to it over SSH.

Understanding our accelerometer readings

Before we jump straight into writing our program, it is probably worth looking at the readings from our accelerometer in a little more detail. If you look closely at the ADXL345 board, you will see that it has two arrows and circle printed on it labelled as **x**, **y**, and **z** respectively. These indicate the axes through which we can measure the movement of the board in relation to the Earth's gravitational pull. This diagram shows a little more clearly how these relate to the rotation of the board through space:

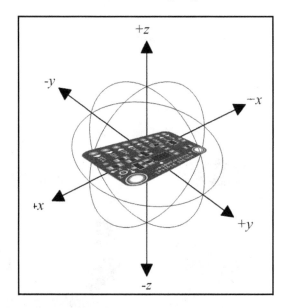

So, let's see how that relates to the different types of movement our head would go through whilst wearing our hat. With your Pi Zero powered up, place the cap upon your head; and then over your SSH connection to the Pi Zero, type the following command, and run the example from the `adxl345-python` directory:

```
python3 ~/WearableTech/Chapter4/adxl345-python/example.py
```

Leave the program running and pay attention to how the values of x, y, and z change as you move your head. If you have installed your ADXL345 and Pi Zero in the same way that I have, then you should see that nodding your head forwards and backwards changes the value of z, leaning your head to either left or right changes the value of x, and raising or lowering your height changes the value of y. Once you are happy after knowing which types of movement change which value, stop the program from running by pressing *Ctrl + C* together.

We are now going to write a Python program, which will take the changing readings of x, y, and z as we move around wearing our hat, and use these to select the colors of our LEDs on our hat. The LEDs on Blinkt are RGB LEDs; this means we need to pass them an **RGB** (**Red, Green, and Blue**) value to tell them what color they should be. Each value for the RGB triplet needs to be in the range of 0 to 255. If you remember, from looking at the output of example.py program we just run, our readings from the ADXL345 range roughly between −1 and 1 on each axis. We will start off our program (after importing the required libraries!) by writing a function that will convert the range of values from the ADXL345 into a valid 0-255 range, ready for our colors to be created. We will then use the value from the y axis to determine how quickly we should reread the data for the colors; this should mean that the faster you are moving, the quicker the colors change:

Back on your SSH connection to your Pi Zero, type the following to move into the Chapter4 directory and make a copy of the adxl345.py library there:

```
cd ~/WearableTech/Chapter4/ && cp ./adxl345-python/adxl345.py ./
```

We are now going to start writing our new Python program in Nano by typing the following:

```
nano ./wearableHat.py
```

Now in Nano, type in the following code:

```
#! /usr/bin/python3

from adxl345 import ADXL345
from time import sleep
from blinkt import set_clear_on_exit, set_pixel, show, set_brightness

adxl345 = ADXL345()

set_clear_on_exit()
set_brightness(0.1)

def adxlToRGB(axis):
    axes = adxl345.getAxes(True)
    absADXL = abs(axes[axis])
    if (absADXL >= 1):
        absADXL = 1
    rgbADXL = int(255 * absADXL)
    return rgbADXL

while True:
    for i in range(8):
        set_pixel(i, adxlToRGB("x"), adxlToRGB("y"), adxlToRGB("z"))
```

```
      show()
  axes = adxl345.getAxes(True)
  sleepY = abs(axes["y"]) / 50
  sleep(sleepY)
```

When you have typed this program, save it and close Nano by pressing *Ctrl + O*, then *Enter* followed by *Ctrl + X*. We can now test whether it works! With your cap still on your head and your Pi Zero powered by a battery pack in your pocket, run the program from your SSH connection by typing:

```
python3 ./wearableHat.py
```

If you walk to a mirror, you should see that the LEDs are changing color depended upon where your head is. Try jumping up and down or jogging on the spot to see what happens!

What did we just do?

So, what did that short program we just wrote actually do? Let's walk through it a line at a time to see.

In line 1, we set up our shebang; this is so we can make it run automatically in the next step, it just tells our computer which interpreter it should use to run the program with and where to find it.

In lines 3-5, we imported the different libraries we need for our program to run. In line 7, we set up a connection to the ADXL345 board. Lines 9 and 10 are from the Blinkt library, and they tell the Blinkt board to clear all of its LEDs when the program closes and to set their brightness to 10%.

Lines 12 through 18 are our custom function to take the readings from ADXL345, and convert them into an integer between 0 and 255, ready to feed to the Blinkt as a RGB value. First, we take the value for the axis, which is passed into the function, and read the current reading from ADXL345. We wrap the output of this with the abs() function. This returns an absolute value, so we know we are not having to deal with negative numbers. Next, we check whether the absolute value of the reading from the ADXL345 is greater than 1 and set to 1 if it is. We then multiply 255 by this value and return an integer of the result using the int() function. This ensures that the returning figure should never be less than 0 or greater than 255.

Lines 20 through 26 are the main program loop. We start a `while True:` loop, which will continue until we stop the program. Next, we start a `for` loop, and tell the program to repeat this loop 8 times, changing the value of `i` each time it goes round the loop. Each time around the loop, we set the pixel `i` with an RGB value based upon the current x, y, and z value of ADXL345 respectively. We then show this pixel and repeat the loop. Once we have completed the loop 8 times, we get the current absolute value of the y axis and divide it by `50`. We then tell the program to sleep for this many seconds before returning to the beginning of the `while True:` loop.

Making our program start automatically

We now need to make our `wearableHat.py` program run automatically when we switch our Pi Zero on. We are going to do this in the same way we did in the previous chapters:

First, we must make the Python program we just wrote executable:

```
chmod +x ./wearableHat.py
```

Now, we will create our service definition file:

```
sudo nano /lib/systemd/system/wearableHat.service
```

Now, type the definition into it:

```
[Unit]
Description=Wearable Hat Service
After=multi-user.target

[Service]
Type=idle        ExecStart=/home/pi/WearableTech/Chapter4/wearableHat.py

[Install]
WantedBy=multi-user.target
```

Save and exit Nano by pressing *Ctrl + O*, followed by *Enter*, and then *Ctrl + X*. Now, change the file permissions, reload the `systemd` daemon and activate our service by typing this:

```
sudo chmod 644 /lib/systemd/system/wearableHat.service
sudo systemctl daemon-reload
sudo systemctl enable wearableHat.service
```

Now, we need to test this is working so reboot your Pi by typing `sudo reboot`, and then when your Pi Zero restarts, you should see that by moving your hat around you get a different color across your Blinkt LEDs. Once you are happy that it is all working correctly, press and hold your power-off button for three seconds to shut your Pi Zero down.

Your motion activated wearable tech hat is now ready to go!

Summary

In this chapter, we looked at adding a new piece of sensor hardware to our Pi Zero; the Adafruit ADXL345. This sensor allowed us to make our project react to it's relative position and movement through the Earth's gravitational fields. You learned how to read the data from this sensor into our Python programs, and then how to connect to and control another piece of hardware called the Blinkt! LED strip. Finally, we installed all of this into a cap and wrote a short Python program to bring it all together.

5
A Tweet-Activated LED T-Shirt

In this project, we will use the skills that we learned in `Chapter 3`, *Sewable LEDs in Clothing*, and take them a little bit further. We are going to create our own personally designed t-shirt using sewable LEDs again but by combining them into our own personal design. We will use a slightly different technique so that the conductive thread is completely hidden, and finally, we will write a Python program that listens to Twitter-awaiting commands to activate our t-shirt!

If you are using the same Pi Zero for this project as you did for the previous project, desolder the four cables, which lead from the Pi Zero to Blinkt; but leave your off-switch and LED in place, as you may need to detach these from the case first. To deactivate the software running automatically, connect to your Pi Zero over SSH and issue the following command:

```
sudo systemctl disable wearableHat.service
```

Once the command completes, you can shut down your Pi Zero by pressing your off-switch button for three seconds. Now, let's look at what we are going to cover in this chapter.

What we will cover

In this chapter, we will cover the following topics:

- What we will need to complete this project
- Creating our t-shirt design
- Adding our LEDs to our item of clothing
- Testing our LEDs
- Writing our main Python program

- Connecting our Pi Zero to the internet
- Making our program run automatically
- Finalizing the garment modifications

Let's jump straight in and look at what parts we will need to complete this project.

The bill of parts

We will make use of the following things in this project:

- A Pi Zero W
- An official Pi Zero case
- A portable battery pack
- Inkjet iron-on transfer paper (A3/A4—two sheets)
- The item of clothing to be modified, for example, a top or t-shirt
- Four red sewable LEDs
- Four green sewable LEDs
- Four blue sewable LEDs
- Conductive threads
- Some fabric, the same color as the clothing
- Thread of the same color as the clothing
- A sewing needle
- Pins
- 15 small metal poppers
- Some black, blue, red, and yellow colored cable
- A mobile phone
- Solders and soldering iron
- Clear nail varnish

Creating our personal t-shirt design

We are going to use an inkjet iron on transfer paper to get our custom design from our computer onto our t-shirt. I will show the design that I have used, but by all means, use your own design here!

You will need to create your image for your t-shirt design in an image editing package. You could use Photoshop if you have access to a copy, but I am going to use **GIMP (GNU Image Manipulation Program)** for my design. There really is not much to worry about here apart from a few points to bear in mind:

- Your final image will need to be reversed. This is especially true if you have any writing in it.
- Think about how you will need to join your LEDs up. We are going to wire up 12 individual LEDs to our Pi Zero and the connections from each cannot cross at any point.
- Your design should fit onto a sheet of A3/A4 paper so that it can be printed onto the transfer sheet.

You can see my final design here. I have included the hashtags that we will configure our project to react to on the design so that people know what to Tweet in order to activate the LEDs. I have four separate hashtags defined. One to activate each set of colors, and a final one, which will activate all colors. As you can see, this design has been reversed so that the text for the hashtags will print the correct way around when transferred onto the garment:

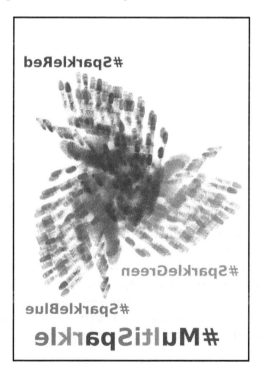

I have then created a second design from this first design, which is a fainter version of the design with some additional markers on it to allow us to see, where the LEDs should be attached and the proposed route that the conductive thread should take. You can see that this design also indicates where the poppers will be attached to connect our Pi to the garment:

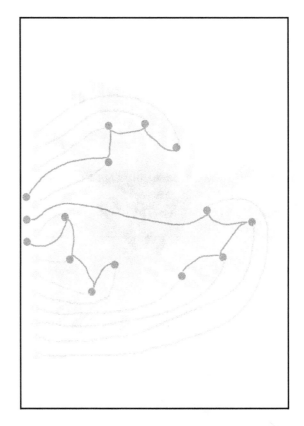

Once you have printed your designs onto your two sheets of transfer paper, iron the full color design onto your garment ensuring you have placed it nicely and centrally on the garment. Now, take your fainter transfer and apply it to the piece of fabric that matches the color of your garment. We will stitch our LEDs to this piece of fabric as opposed to the garment itself. Ensure that you leave enough space around this piece of fabric so that you can hem it and stitch it into the inside of your garment, directly underneath your transferred design. Your piece of fabric also needs to be large enough so that you can fold it back underneath all of the stitching for the LEDs and poppers.

Adding our LEDs to our fabric

In the same way that we stitched the ground or negative connections of our LEDs together in Chapter 3, *Sewable LEDs in Clothing*, we are going to use a common ground connection for all of the negative connections of each color LED. Starting with the red LED furthest from the poppers, place your LED on it's marker on the piece of the fabric and stitch it to the fabric using a long length of conductive thread stitching through the negative connection of the LED. Continue with the same piece of conductive thread, and stitch a running stitch along the marker line on your fabric, and then use this to attach the negative connection of the next LED. Continue doing so for all the red LEDs, and finally, run your conductive thread to a female half of a popper, and stitch this to its marker on the fabric. Finish attaching the popper to fabric by stitching the other three sides down with standard thread. Now, stitch each positive connection of your LEDs to the fabric and run a length of conductive thread to a male popper half on its marker on the fabric; again fasten the other three sides of the popper to the fabric with standard thread. You should now have your four red LEDs stitched to your piece of fabric terminating on five popper studs. Repeat the same process for your green and blue LEDs. To ensure that each LED has a sound connection to the conductive thread, place a small amount of clear nail varnish over each joint of the conductive thread. Here is a picture of my stitched LEDs over the transfer:

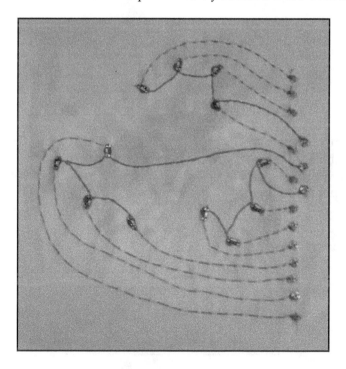

Before we can test our LEDs, we need to create our connection to Pi Zero. In the same way as we did in Chapter 3, *Sewable LEDs in Clothing*, we are going to use a piece of fabric, which will have the other halves of the poppers sewn onto, with a cable soldered to each popper, and at the other end of the cable, it will be soldered to the relevant pin on the Pi Zero. You may have noticed that we have not included a hidden pocket in this design to house the battery and the Pi Zero; this is because I am going to use cables long enough so that the Pi Zero and battery can be placed in the wearers pocket. If you would prefer to have a hidden pocket, then just follow the steps in Chapter 3, *Sewable LEDs in Clothing*.

Cut a length of cable for each popper stud about 50 cm in length. I am cutting three black cables for each ground connection, four red cables for the red LEDs, four blue cables for the blue LEDs, and four yellow cables for the green LEDs. Strip and tin one end of each of your cables, and then solder each cable to its corresponding popper half; male for the black cables and female for the red, blue, and yellow cables. For the black cables, be sure that the cable is soldered across the back of the popper, as shown in this picture, so that the cable does not impact on the closing of the popper. Once you are sure that the popper half, with the cable soldered to it, will securely connect to its counter-part, snip any excess cable from the popper:

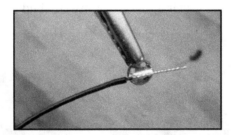

When soldering red, blue, and yellow cables to the female half of the poppers, feed the cable through one of the holes of the popper from the rear, and solder it to the front of the popper half as shown here. Then, clip back any excess cable and check whether it connects soundly to its counter-part popper half:

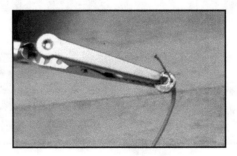

So now that we have soldered the poppers to all of our lengths of cable, we need to attach them to their other halves, and make sure that we can identify which is which and check they are all connected securely. Lay your piece of fabric with the LEDs stitched to it out, and connect each cable to its matching popper. Ensuring that you are running the cables toward the bottom of your design, gently bend each cable so that they run in a line straight down your fabric, as shown here. You can now take a permanent marker or some correction fluid and mark each end of the cables so that you can identify each one later. I am simply placing one to four dots on each of the colored cables to indicate if it is red, blue, or green 1, 2, 3, or 4 LED that it is attached to:

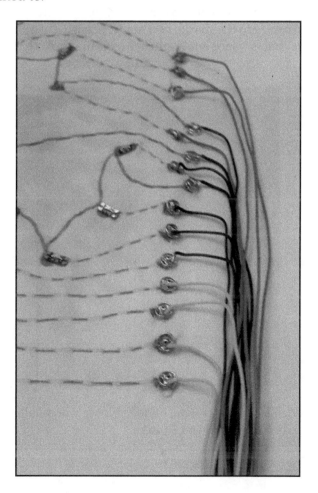

Now that we have labeled our cables, we need to attach them to a piece of fabric so that we can attach and remove them in one go. In the same way we did in Chapter 3, *Sewable LEDs in Clothing*, cut a piece of fabric large enough to cover the poppers and the cables 2.5 times in width. Now, fold the piece of fabric in half and stitch it around one of the long sides and one of the short sides to create a pocket. Once you have stitched the three sides, turn the pocket inside-out and stitch the remaining fourth side. Now, place your stitched piece of fabric over your cables and poppers, and carefully mark the center position of each popper with a marker on your stitched piece of fabric. Now, remove your first popper and cable from the design and stitch it to your piece of fabric. To ensure that the cable does not get damaged, stitch the cable to the fabric too, as shown in this picture. Continue to stitch the remaining poppers and cables to the marks you made, ensuring they are in the correct order! As you add more cables, place a few stitches over the cables to hold them down to the fabric too:

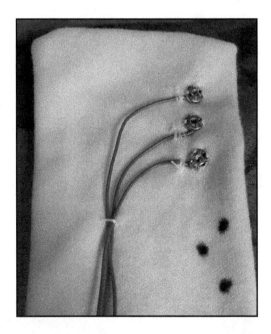

Now that we have stitched all of our poppers and cables to our small piece of fabric, we can neaten the cables up ready to attach to our Pi Zero.

Testing our LEDs

We now need to attach the cables to the correct GPIO points on your Pi Zero. First, you should detach your cables from your LEDs by disconnecting the poppers. Gather all of the cables together and cut them, so they are all about the same length; make sure that you keep your identification markings on each cable! Now, you can cover them in some heat shrink and apply some heat. Each cable now needs to be stripped and tinned, ready to be soldered on to your Pi Zero.

The diagram here shows you which GPIO point to connect which cable to. Feed all the cables through the hole in the bottom of your Pi Zero case, and then carefully solder each one and snip any excess cable using side snips:

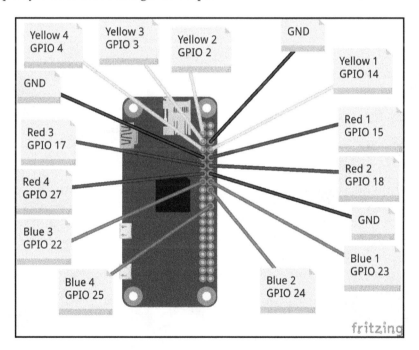

Once we have finished soldering all of your cables to your Pi Zero, we can write a short program to test if they all work. Reconnect your cables to your LEDs, ensuring that you press the poppers down nice and firmly. Now, reinsert your Pi Zero into its case and connect it to a power source. Once it finishes booting up, connect to it over SSH as usual. Move into our project directory by typing, cd ~/WearableTech/, and then make a new directory for this chapter by typing, mkdir Chapter5; now move into our new directory by typing, cd Chapter5.

We are now going to write our short test program in Python to check all the LEDs work as expected. Type `nano LEDtest.py` to open Nano and then type the following code into our new Python file:

```
#! /usr/bin/python3
from gpiozero import LEDBoard
from time import sleep

redLEDs = LEDBoard(15, 18, 17, 27)
greLEDs = LEDBoard(14, 2, 3, 4)
bluLEDs = LEDBoard(23, 24, 22, 25)

while True:
    redLEDs.on()
    sleep(0.5)
    greLEDs.on()
    sleep(0.5)
    bluLEDs.on()
    sleep(0.5)
    redLEDs.off()
    sleep(0.5)
    greLEDs.off()
    sleep(0.5)
    bluLEDs.off()
    sleep(0.5)
    #light the reds in turn
    redLEDs.value = (1, 0, 0, 0)
    sleep(0.25)
    redLEDs.value = (1, 1, 0, 0)
    sleep(0.25)
    redLEDs.value = (1, 1, 1, 0)
    sleep(0.25)
    redLEDs.value = (1, 1, 1, 1)
    sleep(0.25)
    redLEDs.value = (0, 0, 0, 0)
    sleep(0.25)
    #light the greens in turn
    greLEDs.value = (1, 0, 0, 0)
    sleep(0.25)
    greLEDs.value = (1, 1, 0, 0)
    sleep(0.25)
    greLEDs.value = (1, 1, 1, 0)
    sleep(0.25)
    greLEDs.value = (1, 1, 1, 1)
    sleep(0.25)
    greLEDs.value = (0, 0, 0, 0)
    sleep(0.25)
    #light the blues in turn
```

```
bluLEDs.value = (1, 0, 0, 0)
sleep(0.25)
bluLEDs.value = (1, 1, 0, 0)
sleep(0.25)
bluLEDs.value = (1, 1, 1, 0)
sleep(0.25)
bluLEDs.value = (1, 1, 1, 1)
sleep(0.25)
bluLEDs.value = (0, 0, 0, 0)
sleep(0.25)
```

Now, save your file by pressing *Ctrl + O*, followed by *Enter*, and exit Nano by pressing *Ctrl + X*. Now, we need to make our file executable by typing `chmod +x ./LEDtest.py`; now, we can run it by typing `./LEDtest.py`.

All being well, you should see your LEDs light up in a sequence; if any do not work or do not light in the order you expected, then you will need to double check your poppers, stitching, and soldering. You may need to adjust the order of the LEDs in the `LEDBoard` lines to get your LEDs to light in the same order.

Now that we have a tested and working set of LEDs, it is time to move on to writing our main program.

Writing our main Python program

As the title of this chapter suggests, we are going to connect our Python program to Twitter so that different Tweets can control the LEDs on our garment. There are a number of steps involved in doing this. We first need to prepare our Twitter account, so we can connect to it; then we need to install a new Python library and configure it with our Twitter access. Finally, we can write our Python program, which will *listen* to Twitter for our trigger hashtags.

Let's get started straight away!

Preparing your Twitter account

If you do not already have a Twitter account, you are going to want to sign up for one at `ht tps://twitter.com/signup`. Even if you do already have a Twitter account, you may want to sign up for another one, which you can use for testing these kind of projects with so that if you are sending random Tweets out from a program, all of your friends following you will not see them!

Once you have signed up and are logged into your Twitter account visit `https://apps.twitter.com/` to begin setting up your access to Twitter. Click the **Create New App** button to begin. Enter a **Name**, **Description**, and a **Website** for your app; the website can be anything really, but you might want to use your own blog address for example. Your app name will need to be unique, so you might have to try a few different variations. Here you can see what I have entered:

Application Details

Name *

TweetShirt

Your application name. This is used to attribute the source of a tweet and in user-facing authorization screens. 32 characters max

Description *

Twitter reactive LED Pi Zero t shirt

Your application description, which will be shown in user-facing authorization screens. Between 10 and 200 characters max.

Website *

http://www.jonwitts.co.uk

Your application's publicly accessible home page, where users can go to download, make use of, or find out more information about your application. created by your application and will be shown in user-facing authorization screens.

(If you don't have a URL yet, just put a placeholder here but remember to change it later.)

Callback URL

Where should we return after successfully authenticating? OAuth 1.0a applications should explicitly specify their oauth_callback URL on the request t application from using callbacks, leave this field blank.

Scroll to the bottom of the page and select **Yes, I have read and agree to the Twitter Developer Agreement.** Then, click on the **Create your Twitter application** button. Once your app has been created, click on the **Keys and Access Tokens** tab. You should see something like this screenshot. I have blacked out my **Consumer Key** and **Consumer Secret** as you do not want to share these with anyone!

Application Settings

Keep the "Consumer Secret" a secret. This key should never be human-readable in your application.

Consumer Key (API Key) ████████████████████

Consumer Secret (API Secret) ██████████████████████████████

Access Level   Read and write (modify app permissions)

Owner   jonwitts

Owner ID   14441773

Application Actions

Regenerate Consumer Key and Secret   Change App Permissions

If you scroll down a little further, you will see a button labeled **Create my access token**. Click on this, and when the page reloads, you should now have a section on the page like the next screenshot, this time with an **Access Token** and **Access Token Secret**; again I have blacked my keys out in this screenshot:

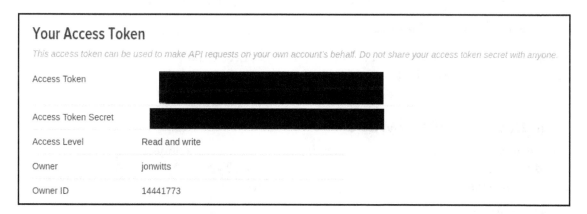

Your Access Token

This access token can be used to make API requests on your own account's behalf. Do not share your access token secret with anyone.

Access Token   ████████████████████████

Access Token Secret   ██████████████████████

Access Level   Read and write

Owner   jonwitts

Owner ID   14441773

We now need to save these four keys into a Python file that we are going to create on our Pi Zero. Due to the length and complexity of these keys, I highly recommend you copy them from the webpage, and paste them into the Python file through your SSH connection; if you try to type them in, you are very likely to make a mistake!

Back on your Pi Zero, stop the test program from running if you have not already by pressing *Ctrl + C* together. You should still be inside the `Chapter5` directory. Create a new file, and open it in Nano by typing `nano auth.py`. Now, type the following into the file, and replacing the keys with the relevant keys from your Twitter application:

```
consumer_key = 'ABCDEFGHIJKLKMNOPQRSTUVWXYZ'
consumer_secret = '1234567890ABCDEFGHIJKLMNOPQRSTUVXYZ'
access_token = 'ZYXWVUTSRQPONMLKJIHFEDCBA'
access_token_secret = '0987654321ZYXWVUTSRQPONMLKJIHFEDCBA'
```

Save the file by pressing *Ctrl + O,* followed by *Enter,* and then exit Nano by pressing *Ctrl + X*. We have now set up our Twitter account ready to be able to connect to it from our Python program.

Installing the Python libraries

We are now going to install a Python library, which will allow us to connect to Twitter. Before we install any new software on our Pi Zero, it is a good idea to check for any updates first. Type the following to update your software package information to install any updates:

```
sudo apt-get update && sudo apt-get upgrade -y
```

Once the upgrade process completes, type the following to install the `twython` library:

```
sudo pip3 install twython
```

We are now ready to connect to Twitter with Python. Let's make a quick test program to check everything is working!

Our first Python Tweet

We are now going to write a short Python program, which will connect to Twitter using our saved tokens from earlier and send a *Hello World* Tweet. Type `nano helloTweet.py` to open a new file in Nano; and now type the following code into it:

```
#! /usr/bin/python3

from twython import Twython

# import our access tokens from the auth.py file
from auth import (
    consumer_key,
```

```
    consumer_secret,
    access_token,
    access_token_secret
)

# make a connection to twitter
twitter = Twython(
    consumer_key,
    consumer_secret,
    access_token,
    access_token_secret
)

# send a hello world tweet
message = "Hello world from my first Python tweet!"
twitter.update_status(status=message)
print("Tweeted: %s" % message)
```

Save the file by pressing *Ctrl + O*, followed by *Enter*, and then exit Nano by pressing *Ctrl + X*. Now, make the file executable by typing `chmod +x helloTweet.py`, and then run it by typing `./helloTweet.py`. You should see something similar to this on your SSH connection:

And if you check out your Twitter profile, you should see a Tweet has been posted similar to this one:

Jon Witts
@jonwitts

Hello world from my first Python tweet!

12:25 AM - 6 Jun 2017

Tweet your reply

If your Tweet did not work, go back and check all of the preceding steps; if your Tweet did work, great! We can now move on to the main program for our project.

Our final program

We are now going to write our final program. This will connect to Twitter and listen for certain hashtags; when it hears the hashtags, our program will activate different LED patterns on our garment.

With your SSH connection to your Pi Zero still open, ensure you are still inside the Chapter5 directory or moving into it if you are not. Now, we will create our blank Python file in Nano by typing nano ledTshirt.py. I will talk through each section of the code as I go; you need to add each section of code together in order to get your final program working. Firstly, we will add the shebang line so that our Pi Zero knows what interpreter should be used to run our program, and then we will import our required Python libraries:

```
#! /usr/bin/python3

# import our libraries
from gpiozero import LEDBoard
from random import randint
from time import sleep

# to listen to Twitter we need the TwythonStreamer library

from twython import TwythonStreamer

# import our access tokens from the auth.py file
from auth import (
    consumer_key,
    consumer_secret,
    access_token,
    access_token_secret
)
```

Now, we will create our four different LEDBoard, one for each colored LED and one for all of them combined. We will also create a function, which we can use to turn our LEDBoard on and off easily. Our function needs to have the name of the LEDBoard passed to it and the number of times to loop. It selects a random number between 0.1 and 0.25 seconds each time it sleeps:

```
# define our LEDBoards
redLEDs = LEDBoard(15, 18, 17, 27)
greLEDs = LEDBoard(14, 2, 3, 4)
bluLEDs = LEDBoard(23, 24, 22, 25)
allLEDs = LEDBoard(redLEDs, greLEDs, bluLEDs)

# define our LED sparkle function
def sparkleLED(board, loop):
```

```
for i in range(loop):
    board.on()
    sleep(randint(10,25)/100)
    board.off()
    sleep(randint(10,25)/100)
```

Now, we will enter into the section of our program, which listens for the different hashtags and triggers the LED patterns. Listening to Twitter is a bit different than posting on Twitter, so we will need to adapt the default `TwythonStreamer` class. We will change what it does on success so that it can react differently to our four hashtags:

```python
# set our hashtags to search for
TERMS = ['#SparkleRed', '#SparkleBlue', '#SparkleGreen', '#MultiSparkle']

# adapt the TwythonStreamer class
class TshirtStreamer(TwythonStreamer):
    def on_success(self, data):
        if 'text' in data:
            if '#SparkleRed' in data['text']:
                sparkleLED(redLEDs, randint(5, 20))
            elif '#SparkleBlue' in data['text']:
                sparkleLED(bluLEDs, randint(5, 20))
            elif '#SparkleGreen' in data['text']:
                sparkleLED(greLEDs, randint(5, 20))
            else:
                sparkleLED(allLEDs, randint(5, 20))

# connect with our streamer class
stream = TshirtStreamer(
    consumer_key,
    consumer_secret,
    access_token,
    access_token_secret
)
stream.statuses.filter(track=TERMS)
```

Now, save our file by pressing *Ctrl* + *O* followed by *Enter*, and then exit Nano by pressing *Ctrl* + *X*. Now, make your program executable by typing `chmod +x ./ledTshirt.py`.

You can now test that your program is listening for your hashtags by sending some Tweets with different hashtags in them and watch your LEDs light up. Type `./ledTshirt.py` to run your program and then Tweet away! Once you are happy everything is working as expected, press *Ctrl* + *C* to stop your program from running.

Connecting our Pi Zero to the internet

So, we have our Pi Zero listening to Twitter and lighting up our LEDs on our desk at home, but what if we want to wear our t-shirt out and about and have it still work? To make this work, we are going to need to connect our Pi Zero to some form of mobile Internet connection. There are many ways in which we could do this, but the easiest, by far, is to make use of the mobile data on our smart phone and create a mobile hotspot between our smart phone and our Pi Zero.

The method of doing this for each smart phone will vary slightly, and if you do not know how to do it with your type of phone, a quick Google search should yield the results you need. Once you have set up a mobile hotspot on your phone, you will need to take note of the network name or SSID of your hotspot and the password or key.

With those two pieces of information recorded, we are going to edit our Pi Zero configuration so that if it sees our mobile hotspot Wi-Fi. It will connect to it rather than our home Wi-Fi we set up at the beginning of the book. Turn off the hotspot on your phone and connect to your Pi Zero via SSH if you are not already.

Type `sudo nano /etc/wpa_supplicant/wpa_supplicant.conf` to open the Wi-Fi network configuration file in Nano. You should see something like this:

```
network={
    ssid="myhomenetwork"
    psk="0123456789ABCDEF"
}
```

Here, `ssid` is the network name of your home Wi-Fi network and `psk` is the password. We need to add a new line to this network configuration, and then add a completely new network configuration underneath this one. Adjust your file so it looks like this, obviously replacing the parts between double quote marks with the correct details for your Wi-Fi networks. The `priority` line indicates which network should take priority, the higher the number the more desirable it is:

```
network={
    ssid="myhomenetwork"
    psk="0123456789ABCDEF"
    priority=5
}

network={
    ssid="mymobilehotspot"
    psk="0123456789ABCDEF"
    priority=10
}
```

Save the file by pressing *Ctrl + O* followed by *Enter*, and then exit Nano by pressing *Ctrl + X*. You can now switch off your Pi Zero by holding your power button in for three seconds, and then removing the power lead. Once your Pi Zero is powered off, turn the mobile hotspot on on your smart phone, and then power your Pi Zero back up. You should be able to see from the hotspot settings on your phone that your PI zero has connected to your smart phone's hotspot rather than your home Wi-Fi. Here is what my Mobile hotspot screen looks like when my Pi Zero is connected to it:

Once you are happy that your Pi Zero is connecting to your mobile hotspot, switch it off again and turn off the hotspot on your smart phone. You can now switch your Pi Zero back on and connect to it again over SSH through your home Wi-Fi network.

Making our program start automatically

As with our previous projects, we now need to make our program start as soon as we switch our Pi Zero on:

Now, we will create our service definition file; type this:

```
sudo nano /lib/systemd/system/twitterTshirt.service
```

Now, type the definition into it:

```
[Unit]
Description=Twitter TShirt Service
After=multi-user.target

[Service]
Type=idle
ExecStart=/home/pi/WearableTech/Chapter5/ledTshirt.py

[Install]
WantedBy=multi-user.target
```

Save and exit Nano by typing *Ctrl + O*, followed by *Enter*, and then *Ctrl + X*. Now, change the file permissions, reload the `systemd` daemon, and activate our service by typing this:

```
sudo chmod 644 /lib/systemd/system/twitterTshirt.service
sudo systemctl daemon-reload
sudo systemctl enable twitterTshirt.service
```

Now, we need to test if this is working, so reboot your Pi by typing `sudo reboot`, and then when your Pi Zero restarts, you should be able to send it a Tweet and see the LEDs light up. Once you are happy that it is all working correctly, press and hold your power-off button for three seconds to shut your Pi Zero down.

Finalizing the garment modifications

The last thing we have to do now is to add our LEDs into our printed t-shirt design. Turn your printed t-shirt inside out, and then take your piece of fabric with your LEDs stitched into it and place it on top of the design of the t-shirt with the LEDs facing the t-shirt. Take some time to ensure that the two designs line up nicely and pin it in place. I then folded the fabric back over the back of the LED stitching so that none of the conductive thread would come into contact with the wearer's skin. With everything pinned in place, sew three sides of the design onto the t-shirt. I used a sewing machine to do this, but you could do it by hand if you do not have access to a sewing machine. Be sure to leave the side of the design closest to where your cables attach to the poppers open so that you can attach and detach the Pi Zero from your design. When everything is stitched in place, trim any excess fabric and thread, and turn your garment the right-way-round again.

You can now reattach your cables to your t-shirt and power on your Pi Zero. If you want your t-shirt to work away from your home Wi-Fi, ensure that you turn on your phone's mobile hotspot before you switch on your Pi Zero.

You are now ready to have your t-shirt LEDs activated by Twitter! Send a Tweet containing any of the hashtags printed on your design, and see your LEDs light up in response! Here is a picture of my t-shirt reacting to the `#MultiSparkle` hashtag and a link to a video on YouTube (`https://www.youtube.com/watch?v=XfbSxf918ZQ`) where you can see it reacting to the different hashtags:

Summary

In this chapter, we have developed our skills of using sewable LEDs further, and also incorporated them with a printed design on our garment. You have also learned how to connect to Twitter using Python and make our programs react to different phrases or hashtags found on Twitter. Finally, you learned how to connect our Pi Zero to different Wi-Fi networks using the priority keyword in our `wpa_supplicant` file. This final step allows us to now take our wearable projects out and about with us when they need an Internet connection.

In our next project, we will be making a LED laptop bag. We will make use of a RGB addressable LED strip to create a matrix of programmable LEDs across the front of our bag. We will then create the necessary electronic circuits to control these with our Pi Zero and also write our Python program to control our LED bag design.

6
An LED Laptop Bag

In this project, we will attach an Adafruit DotStar LED strip to the front of a laptop bag, and we will then conceal our Pi Zero, the extra electronic devices required to control the LEDs, as well as all of the batteries required to run everything inside the pocket of the bag. Using Python, we will then write a program that will control our fully-colored, programmable LED strip to create different multicolored patterns on the front of our bag.

If you are using the same Pi Zero for this project as you did for the previous project, desolder the 15 cables that lead from the Pi Zero to the LEDs on the t-shirt, but leave your off switch and LED in place, as you may need to detach these from the case first. To deactivate the software running automatically, connect to your Pi Zero over SSH and issue the following command:

```
sudo systemctl disable twitterTshirt.service
```

Once the command completes, you can shut down your Pi Zero by pressing your off switch for three seconds. Now, let's look at what we are going to cover in this chapter.

What we will cover

In this chapter, we will cover the following topics:

- Creating our electrical circuit
- Controlling our LED strip with Python
- Adding our LED strip to the bag
- Writing our main Python program
- Making our program run automatically

Let's get on with things straight away and look at what we will need to complete this project.

The bill of parts

We will make use of the following things in this project:

- A Pi Zero W
- An official Pi Zero case
- A portable USB battery pack with 2 A output (as high a mAh as you can find)
- A portable USB battery pack for your Pi Zero
- An Adafruit DotStar Black 144 LED 1 m strip
- An Adafruit Perma-Proto quarter size
- 74AHCT125 – Quad Level-Shifter (3V to 5V)
- A 14 pin 0.3" IC socket
- Solid core cable—black
- Stranded core cable—red, black, yellow, and blue
- Stranded core cable, 18 AWG size, red, and black
- DIY USB male socket
- Cable heat shrink
- Small anti-static bag
- A plain colored laptop bag
- A Velcro to match your laptop bag in color
- Soldering iron and solders
- A hot glue gun
- Volt meter

Creating our electrical circuit

Before we go any further with this project, we need to talk a little bit about power for our DotStar LED strip. DotStar LEDs have a very specific power requirement; if there is not enough power, you will not be able to see them clearly; and if there's too much power, you risk damaging your LEDs. To complicate matters further, we need our power source to be portable in this project, so we will need to make use of batteries of one kind or another. Due to the exacting power requirements of the DotStar LEDs, we will also need to use some electronics to allow our Pi Zero to control DotStar LEDs.

DotStar LEDs are rated as 5V devices. Including a +- 10% tolerance gives us a safe working voltage range of 4.5V to 5.5V to power our DotStar LEDs. Now, you may ask why we don't just use the 5V line from the Pi Zero to power the LED strip? The reason is due to the amount of power the LED strip can draw. When lighting all of the LEDs in our strip, the power draw would be too much for our Pi Zero, and we would risk damaging it. Therefore, we will use a separate battery pack to power our LED strip. The other complication with using 5V LEDs, such as the DotStars, is that the GPIO pins from the PI Zero are rated at 3.3V, therefore we ideally need to step up their voltage to 5V before trying to use them to control the DotStar LEDs. This is where the 74AHCT125 comes into play.

Here is the completed wiring diagram for our project. There is a lot going on in this, so I will talk it through one section at a time:

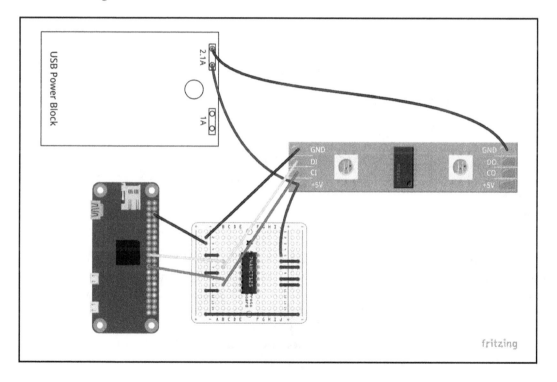

First of all, let's take a look at the Perma-Proto board and the wiring on there. The first thing you will need to do is solder your 14 pin IC socket across the center section of your Perma-Proto board. I could not find 14 pin IC sockets, so I ended up using a 20 pin socket. We now need to connect up the common ground lines from our chip to the common ground rails of the board. Use your solid core black cable and join the sockets together as shown by the diagram here:

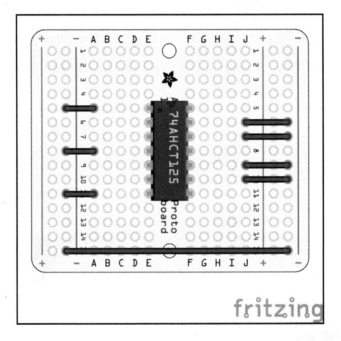

When you are soldering, be sure that you do not have your 74AHCT125 chip inserted in your IC socket, but pay attention to where the top of the chip is marked with the semicircular inset in the chip. What we have done here is join both ground rails to each other, and then to connect pins 1, 4, 7, 9, 10, 12, and 13 of our IC chip to the ground also. You can read the schematic of the 75AHCT125 chip at: https://cdn-shop.adafruit.com/product-files/1787/1787AHC125.pdf. The reason for connecting pins 9 and 12 to ground is because we will not be making use of them in this project.

We can now look at the connections to our Pi Zero. DotStar LEDs require two data connections to our Pi Zero and will make use of the Pi's SPI interface. Each data connection needs to communicate with the DotStar LEDs at 5V, so we will input our data lines from the Pi Zero into the 75AHCT125 chip, allowing it to up their voltage to match the DotStar LEDs before outputting to the DotStar. We will also connect our common ground rail back to a ground pin on our Pi Zero so that all devices use a common ground in our circuit.

Take a length of black, blue, and yellow stranded cable, about 15 cm in length, and strip and tin each end. You then need to solder them to the Perma-Proto board and Pi Zero as shown here:

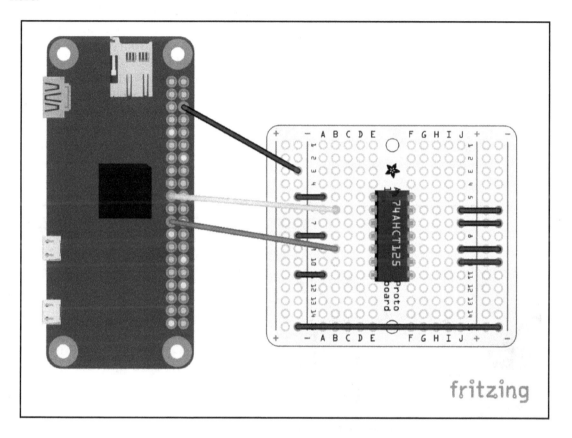

When soldering the cables to your Pi Zero, feed them through the hole in the back of the Pi Zero case and solder them to the Pi Zero from behind. To keep things neat and tidy, you can wrap these cables in a length of heat shrink before attaching them to your Pi Zero. Now, we need to connect the DotStar LED strip into our circuit. First of all, you will need to carefully remove the plastic casing from your DotStar strip, taking care not to damage any of the LEDs in the process. You will now need to desolder the cables from each end of the DotStar strip so that we can add our own. Cut lengths of about 45 cm of blue, yellow, black, and red stranded cable, stripping and tinning each end. You can then solder them to the Perma-Proto board and the end of the DotStar strip as shown here. Be careful to ensure you are soldering these cables to the end of the DotStar strip with the arrows pointing away from it. Again, you can wrap these four cables in a length of heat shrink to keep them tidy. We have now finished all our soldering on the Perma-Proto board, so we can insert our 74AHCT125 chip now, ensuring the semi-circular inset on the chip is lined up with row 5 on the board:

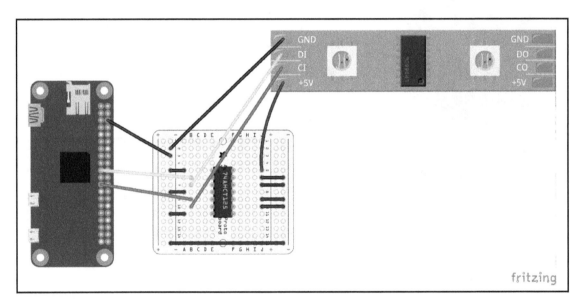

The only part of our electronics which is left is to provide power to the DotStar LED strip. As you can see from the completed wiring diagram, we are going to make use of a portable USB battery block for this. It is important that it is the one that has a 2 A output and is as high an mAh rating as you can get. The one I am using is rated at 10,400 mAh.

We now need to make a custom USB cable to power our DotStar strip with. Take a 60 cm length of the red and black 18 AWG stranded cable and strip and tin each end. We are using a heavy gauge cable here, as DotStar LEDs can pull a lot of current when they are running, and the thin cables inside standard USB leads will not be able to supply sufficient power.

Solder your red and black cables to the USB insert as shown in the image here. I had to file the channel, which the cables run out of on both parts of the case, to get it to close around the two cables:

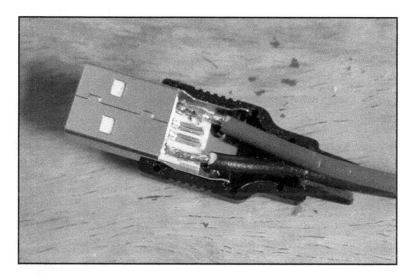

It is worth checking if the polarity is correct by putting a volt meter across the other two ends of your cables and plugging your USB plug into your battery pack. At this point, just wrap your USB plug and cables in some electrical tape to secure everything, as we will be adjusting this later on.

You now need to solder the other end of your red and black USB cable to your DotStar LED strip as shown in the previous image. You are connecting the red (positive) cable to the same point as the positive cable going back to your Perma-Proto board and the black cable (ground) to the ground connection at the other end of the DotStar LED strip. Solder them carefully, ensuring that you do not disturb the positive cable back to the Perma-Proto board in the process.

Controlling our LED strip with Python

Now that we have completed all of our electronics, we can test that we can control our DotStar LED strip using the Python programming language. Switch on your Pi Zero and connect to it via SSH as normal. First off, we will create a directory for all of our code for this chapter; type `mkdir ~/WearableTech/Chapter6`; and then move into the directory by typing `cd ~/WearableTech/Chapter6`.

We now need to enable the SPI interface on our Pi Zero. Start the Raspberry Pi Configuration tool by typing `sudo raspi-config`. From the menu that opens, select **5 Interfacing Options**, and then in the sub menu select **P4 SPI**; then press tab to highlight **Enable**. Press *Enter* twice and then restart your Pi Zero by typing `sudo reboot now`.

Once your Pi Zero has rebooted, connect to it via SSH again, move into your newly created Chapter6 directory and then issue the following command:

```
git clone https://github.com/adafruit/Adafruit_DotStar_Pi
```

We have now cloned the Adafruit DotStar Python library to let us control our LEDs. Check that you have your DotStar set up as per the diagram in the previous section and that they are powered on using your USB battery pack. Now on your Pi Zero, move into the newly cloned git repository by typing `cd Adafruit_DotStar_Pi`. We now need to edit the provided test file to work with our DotStar strip. Type `nano strandtest.py` and look for this line early in the code:

```
numpixels = 30 # Number of LEDs in strip
```

Change `30` to the `144`, and then a few lines down, look for this:

```
strip = Adafruit_DotStar(numpixels, datapin, clockpin)
```

Now, change it to this:

```
strip = Adafruit_DotStar(numpixels, 12000000)
```

This is `12` followed by six zeros (12 million). Save the changes by pressing *Ctrl + O*, followed by *Enter*, and then exit Nano by pressing *Ctrl + X*. We can now run this test file by typing this:

```
python strandtest.py
```

Notice that we are using Python 2 here, not Python 3. This is because the DotStar library from Adafruit is not compiled against Python 3. If all of your wiring and soldering in the previous section is working, then you will see a set of ten LEDs chase down the length of the strip; first red, then green, then blue, then going back to the beginning and running again (or until you press *Ctrl + C*). Let it run, watch closely, and make sure every LED along the strip lights all three colors. If your LEDs are not lighting up as described, then go back and double check your electronics or failing that you can check the *Troubleshooting* section of this Adafruit setup guide at: `https://learn.adafruit.com/dotstar-pi-painter/asse mbly-part-1#troubleshooting`, or head over to their support forums and post a question at: `https://forums.adafruit.com/`.

With my DotStar LED strip, the colors were not in the correct order (red, then blue, then green), so I edited the `strandtest.py` file again and changed my strip declaration to this:

```
strip = Adafruit_DotStar(numpixels, 12000000, order='bgr')
```

You may need to adjust the b, g, and r order to get your colors displaying correctly.

Adding our LED strip to the bag

We now need to attach our LED strip to our laptop bag. We are going to cut the strip into six smaller strips of 24 LEDs each. We will then solder cables to join the points back together to create a LED matrix, which we will attach to the front of our bag using Velcro.

Start by very carefully cutting your LED strip just after the 24th LED. You can use sharp scissors for this, but be sure to cut through the center of the four copper solder pads. Now, cut 5 lengths of your yellow and blue stranded cable and 5 lengths of your red and black 18 AWG cable. The length needs to be enough to join the LED strip back together; mine were about 5 cm. Once you have cut all of your lengths of cable, strip and tin each end.

Now, turn your LED strips over and secure the piece you are soldering to and your cable you are soldering with a pair of helping hands. To solder your cables to the copper pads on the strips, first add a small amount of solder to the pad, then heat again and present your cable to the solder. It should then attach. I found it easier to solder the cable to the half pad at an angle, so it lay across the cut of the pad. This picture shows me in the process of soldering one of my joints:

Now, solder these cables to the other part of the LED strip, ensuring that you match up the power, ground, data, and clock cables and that you keep the arrows on the strip going in the same direction. I found it useful to bend the heavy gauge cables first before soldering. After I completed each joint, I then resoldered the main ground cable to the end of my strip, powered on my Pi Zero and ran the `strandtest.py` file to check whether it was still working as expected. Once I had confirmed that my joint was good I trimmed any excess cable with side-snips, and then provided some strain relief to the cables by spreading some hot glue across the cables to the back of the LED strip. To keep my strips lined up nicely, I used some Blu-Tack to hold the cables in place as you can see in this picture:

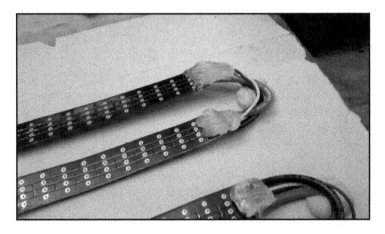

Once you have completed reattaching all six strips, you can turn them over and apply a little hot glue on the joints to the cables, taking care not to get any glue on your LEDs. This picture shows you my completed matrix with the strand test program running on it:

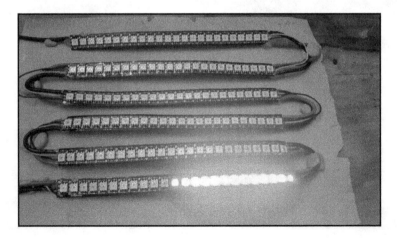

We can now do a little bit of tidying up of our cables back to the Pi Zero and the USB battery, and then look at attaching our LED matrix to our bag.

Unwrap the electrical tape from your DIY USB plug, and detach your cables from inside it. You can now bring the ground cable neatly up to the point where the live cable connects to the LED matrix, running it along the ends of the LED strips. Place a small piece of tape around the two cables at this point to keep them together; you can then cut the cables so they are an equal length from this point, and then insert them into a length of heat shrink, heat the heat shrink, and then resolder your cables into your DIY USB plug. The total length of this cable probably does not need to be more than 30 cm. Plug your USB cable into your battery and check that you are getting the expected voltage across the two cables you just soldered into your USB plug. To finish your USB plug off, apply some hot glue inside the case to hold the two pieces together, and then wrap the case and cables with some electrical tape to secure them.

We will now adjust the length of the cables between the DotStar strip and the Perma-Proto board to match your USB power cable. Desolder the cables from the Perma-Proto board; trim them to the same length as your USB power cables, and then strip and tin the ends, but do not reattach them to the Perma-Proto board yet.

You now need to turn the whole LED matrix over so that the LEDs are facing down. Now, cut the lengths of the sewable Velcro that are long enough to cover each strip of LEDs. You can attach this to your LED strips using hot glue. Once this has dried, and you are happy that you have a strong bond, turn your LED matrix over and tidy up any strings of hot glue. You can now position the LEDs in front of your laptop bag. My laptop bag has a pocket on the front of it, so I will be attaching the LED matrix to this pocket. Align it nicely and centrally, and then mark either end of the Velcro strip on the bag. Repeat this for all six strips, and then take them away from the bag. You need to also mark where the USB power cables and cable to the Perma-Proto board are going to feed through the bag, as we are going to cut a small hole here, large enough to feed our USB plug through.

Once you are happy you have marked the position of all six Velcro strips in the correct place and know where your two cables are going to feed back into the bag from, you can attach the Velcro to the laptop bag using hot glue. This will be easiest if you detach the half of the Velcro strip from the LED strip first, as this will allow you to get a really good bond between the strip and the bag. Once the glue has set, carefully attach your LED strips to the bag, and feed the two cables through the hole.

You can now resolder the cables to the Perma-Proto board in the same location as they were before. At this point, it would be a good idea to connect your Pi Zero up to power, plug in your USB battery for the LEDs and check the `strandtest.py` file still works as expected. If all is working as expected, you can now place your Perma-Proto bag into the small anti-static bag and place the Perma-Proto board, Pi Zero, and USB battery packs inside the pocket. Here is a picture of my laptop bag with the LEDs attached and the `strandtest.py` program running too!

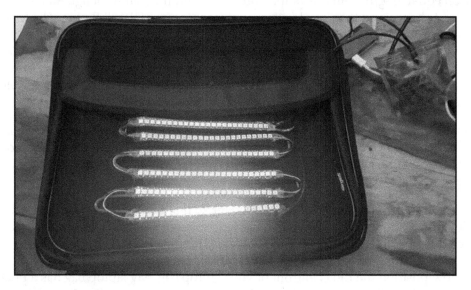

We are now ready to start to program our LED matrix patterns!

Writing our main Python program

Connect your USB battery to the LED matrix and power up your Pi Zero, and then connect to your Pi Zero via SSH. Move into the `Adafruit_DotStar_Pi` directory by typing this:

```
cd ~/WearableTech/Chapter6/Adafruit_DotStar_Pi
```

We are going to make our Python program in this directory as it contains the necessary files to connect to the DotStar strip with Python. Open a new file in Nano by typing this:

```
nano ledBag.py
```

In the empty file that opens, type the following:

```
#! /usr/bin/python

import time
from random import randint
from dotstar import Adafruit_DotStar

# set up our strip
numpixels = 144
strip = Adafruit_DotStar(numpixels, 12000000, order='bgr')

# start our strip
strip.begin()
strip.setBrightness(32)
```

In this first section of our program, we are importing our required libraries, setting up the details for our strip, and the initializing the strip. In the next section of the program we will define three functions: one to clear all of the pixels when we finish a pattern, and two functions for different types of LED patterns across our strip. Continue adding the following to the end of your `ledBag.py` file:

```
def finish():
    # finished, clear the pixels
    strip.clear()
    strip.show()

def wormChase(startLength):
    # start with a chase like the strandtest
    # but with the chase getting longer each time
    head = 0
    tail = -startLength
    color = 0xFF0000
    # repeat nine times across all pixels
    for i in range(numpixels * 9):
        strip.setPixelColor(head, color)
        strip.setPixelColor(tail, 0)
        strip.show()
        time.sleep(1.0 / 50)
        head += 1
        if(head >= numpixels):
            head = 0
            color >>= 8
            tail = tail - 3
            if(color == 0): color = 0xFF0000
        tail += 1
        if(tail >= numpixels): tail = 0
```

```
def colWipe(startR, startG, startB, colInc):
    # move a column across the matrix
    colEven = [0, 48, 96]
    colOdd = [47, 95, 143]
    r = startR
    g = startG
    b = startB

    for i in range(24):
        for i in colEven:
            strip.setPixelColor(i, r, g, b)
            strip.show()
        for i in colOdd:
            strip.setPixelColor(i, r, g, b)
            strip.show()
        # pause
        time.sleep(1.0 / 50)
        # increase colEven
        colEven = [x+1 for x in colEven]
        # decrease colOdd
        colOdd = [x-1 for x in colOdd]
        # change colour
        if r + colInc < 255:
            r = r + colInc
        elif g + colInc < 255:
            g = g + colInc
        elif b + colInc < 255:
            b = b + colInc
    time.sleep(0.5)
```

So, we have declared three functions; `finish()`, `wormChase()`, and `colWipe()`.

The `wormChase()` function is almost the same as the program in the `strandtest.py` file, except we can now pass a starting length to it, rather than it always chasing 10 pixels down the length of the LED strip. The length of the LEDs also gets longer each time it runs.

The `colWipe()` function takes four parameters; a starting value for the red, green, and blue values, and a value which we will use to increment the color values by as the we move across the columns of LEDs on our matrix.

The final function, `finish()`, just switches off all the LEDs for us.

We now need to write the main loop of our program, which will call these functions. We are going to use a try and except format so that if we use *Ctrl + C* to stop our program from running, it will turn off all the LEDs before exiting. Add the following code to the end of your ledBag.py file:

```
try:
    while True:
        wormChase(randint(5,48))
        finish()
        for i in range(3):
            colWipe(randint(1,50), randint(1,50), randint(1,50),
randint(5,64))
            finish()
except KeyboardInterrupt:
    finish()
```

To ensure that our patterns are slightly different every time they run, we are using the randint() function to select a random number within a suitable range, for each of our parameters.

Save the file by pressing *Ctrl + O*, followed by *Enter*, and then exit Nano by pressing *Ctrl + X*. Now, we will make the file executable by typing this:

```
sudo chmod+x ./ledBag.py
```

Now test that your file works by typing the following:

```
./ledBag.py
```

Let it run through a few times so that you are sure the random number selection is working. When you are happy that it is working, press *Ctrl + C* to stop the program from running (notice that all the LEDs turn off).

Making our program start automatically

As with our previous projects, we now need to make our program start as soon as we switch our Pi Zero on.

First we will create our service definition file:

```
sudo nano /lib/systemd/system/ledBag.service
```

Now, type the definition into it:

```
[Unit]
Description=LED Laptop Bag Service
After=multi-user.target

[Service]
Type=idle
ExecStart=/home/pi/WearableTech/Chapter6/Adafruit_DotStar_Pi/ledBag.py

[Install]
WantedBy=multi-user.target
```

Save and exit Nano by typing *Ctrl + O*, followed by *Enter*, and then *Ctrl + X*. Now, change the file permissions, reload the `systemd` daemon, and activate our service by typing this:

```
sudo chmod 644 /lib/systemd/system/ledBag.service
sudo systemctl daemon-reload
sudo systemctl enable ledBag.service
```

Now, we need to test if this is working so reboot your Pi by typing `sudo reboot`; and then when your Pi Zero restarts, you should see your LED matrix start to display your patterns. When you want to stop your display from running, you can press and hold your power button on your Pi Zero for three seconds, and then disconnect the USB plug, which is powering the DotStar strip. You can see a short video of the LEDs running on my completed bag at `https://youtu.be/TfTaTMSzMY0`.

Summary

In this chapter, you learned the necessary electronics to get our 3.3V Pi Zero to control 5V items, and also we have done some pretty tricky soldering to cut and rejoin our DotStar LED strip into a matrix.

We looked at ways of attaching electrical components to fabrics, which we have not used before and also had to think in a bit more detail about our portable power sources!

We have finished up with a truly portable, and even if I say so myself, quite a stunning new bag for our laptop to be transported around in!

In the next chapter, we are going to be learning about Python programming in a little more detail, as we make use of our Pi Zero to create our own pedometer.

7
Creating Your Own Pedometer

In this project, we will attach an Adafruit Triple-Axis Accelerometer and a Pimoroni Scroll pHAT HD to our Pi Zero and write a Python program so that we can count the number of steps we take while wearing the Pi Zero. We will then scroll the current number of steps across our Scroll pHAT HD.

If you are using the same Pi Zero for this project as you did for the previous project, desolder the three cables which attach the Pi Zero to the Perma-Proto board, but leave your off switch and LED in place, as you may need to detach these from the case first. To deactivate the software running automatically, connect to your Pi Zero over SSH and issue the following command:

```
sudo systemctl disable ledBag.service
```

Once the command completes, you can shut down your Pi Zero by pressing the off switch for three seconds. Now, let's look at what we are going to cover in this chapter.

What we will cover

In this chapter, we will cover the following topics:

- How a pedometer works
- Setting up our hardware
- Counting steps with Python
- Making our program run automatically

Let's get on with the things straight away and look at what we will need to complete this project.

The bill of parts

We will make use of the following things in this project:

- A Pi Zero W
- An official Pi Zero case (with the camera lid)
- A portable USB battery pack for your Pi Zero
- An Adafruit ADXL345 Triple Axis Accelerometer
- A Pimoroni Scroll pHAT HD
- Stranded core cable – red, black, yellow, and blue
- Cable heat shrink
- Soldering iron and solders
- A hot glue gun

How a pedometer works

Before we begin looking at our hardware or Python program for this project, it is worth spending a little bit of time understanding how a pedometer uses the data from an accelerometer to calculate steps taken. If you already use a pedometer and have compared the results from one application or device to that of another, you are probably aware that they will nearly always differ in their readings. This is because each pedometer will be using a slightly different algorithm to calculate steps taken from the data it is receiving from the accelerometer.

Our accelerometer measures acceleration through three different axis, **x, y**, and **z**, and it returns these as a measurement relative to the gravitational pull upon the device.

This image displays the three axis of movement which our accelerometer can detect:

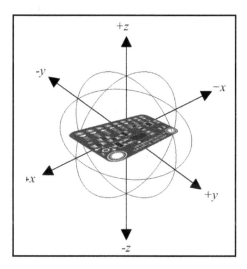

Now, if we think about how a person walks, they bounce up and down as they take each step. If you were to watch the top of someone's head as they walked along, you would see it rose and fell with every step that they took. If our person was holding their accelerometer as shown in the preceding diagram, and they were moving in the direction of **y**, we could measure their number of steps by counting the peaks in the rise and fall of the acceleration along the **z** axis. In a perfect world that would plot a lovely, clean sine wave where we could measure the number of peaks to give us our number of steps, as shown in this plot:

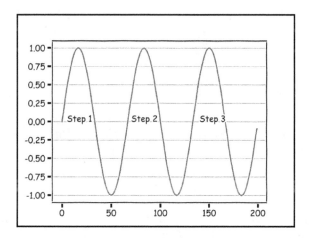

Of course, we do not live in an ideal world, so to accurately measure a persons steps from the movement of an accelerometer is not really this straight forward. If you are using the pedometer app on your smart phone, for example, it is unlikely that your phone will be in a certain orientation or even remain in the same orientation whilst you move around. This will mean that you would need to measure the data from all three axis and combine them together. You would also need to calculate what the force applied to each axis from the normal gravitational pull of the earth was, and subtract it from our complete data set to be left with the user's gravitational change over time. You would then have to combine this 3D data set into a 1D data set so that we could plot our chart to measure the peaks. It doesn't stop here though! You would also then need to perform various filters upon your data to clean it up and remove any extraneous data. There is a lot of really quite interesting math involved in this whole process, and it is well worth a read if you are interested in how pedometers are made and why each one might record a slightly different step count. This website has some really good information on it, `http://www.aosabook.org/en/500L/a-pe dometer-in-the-real-world.html`.

However, to try to build such an accurate pedometer is well beyond the scope of a single chapter in this book, so we are going to make a few decisions which will enable us to write a far simpler program that will act as our pedometer:

1. We will position the accelerometer in a particular orientation.
2. We will secure our Pi Zero to our clothing in a certain orientation.
3. We will use an upper threshold level to decide when a step has been taken.

These three steps will mean that we will be able to get a reasonable step count without needing to go into some very complex mathematics and Python code to achieve it. Before we get started with the Python. Let's look at setting our hardware up.

Setting up our hardware

So, the next thing to do is to get our hardware set up. We are going to make use of the same Adafruit ADXL345 accelerometer we used in our *A Motion-Reactive LED Cap* project; and to display the details of the steps taken so far, we will make use of the same Pimoroni Scroll pHAT HD that we used in the *Scrolling LED Badge* project. Both of these devices use the I2C protocol to communicate with our Pi Zero. The I2C protocol was designed to get around some of the problems with connecting multiple devices to an asynchronous serial port or an SPI port. I2C allows you to connect (over short distances) multiple devices through the same bus. Each device connected to the I2C bus must identify itself with a unique device ID.

Thankfully, our ADXL345 and Scroll pHAT HD are set to use different IDs already. This means we can connect them to the same I2C bus on our Pi Zero without any reconfiguration. If you want to read a bit more about the I2C protocol and how it works, this is a good place to start, `https://learn.sparkfun.com/tutorials/i2c`.

Let's get started by preparing the cables we will need for our project:

1. Cut a 10 cm length of red, blue, yellow, and black cable.
2. Cut a 30 cm length of red, blue, yellow, and black cable.
3. Strip and tin one end of all these cables.
4. Strip and tin the other end of the red and black cables.
5. Take the end of the blue and yellow cables that have not been tinned and twist them tightly together.
6. Tin each of these double twisted cables as shown here:

We are now going to connect the cables to our Scroll pHAT HD ADXL345 and our Pi Zero. As the Scroll pHAT HD is a 5V device, and we need to run the ADXL345 at 3.3V for it to work with the Pi Zero, we are going to provide each device with a ground and voltage line of its own. The wiring diagram for the two devices is shown here:

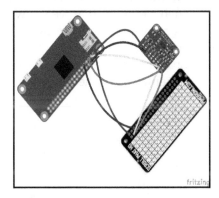

We are going to install our ADXL345 inside our lid of our Pi Zero case again, and then attach the Scroll pHAT HD to our clothing using a pin as we did with the *Scrolling LED Badge*. To do this, we will make use of the lid, which comes with the official Pi Zero case that has a hole in the middle of it for the Pi camera. We will glue the ADXL345 into the lid, and then run the cables for the Scroll pHAT HD through the camera hole so that we can attach our Scroll pHAT HD to our clothes.

Solder the single ends of the four shorter cables to Pi Zero as shown. Solder them to the front of the Pi Zero so that the cables come into the case rather than through the back. We are attaching the red cable to the 3.3V hole, the black cable to the ground hole on pin 6, the yellow cable to the I2C Data SDA on pin 3, and the blue cable to the I2C clock SCL on pin 5. Now, take your longer black and red cables and attach them to the Pi Zero on pins 2 and 9 as shown in the following picture. Trim any excess cable from the back of your Pi Zero with a pair of side snips.

We are now ready to attach our ADXL345 to our shorter cables as shown in the following picture. Solder each of the four shorter cables into their correct holes from the front of the ADXL345, snipping off any excess cables with side snips when completed. To get the double yellow and blue cables through and soldered neatly, I found that I had to snip the twisted cable first to get a nice neat end, and then apply a little heat to the cables with my soldering iron while pulling them through with a pair of long-nosed pliers.

We are now going to take the four remaining cables and solder them to our Scroll pHAT HD. First take the cables and feed them through the hole in the top of the Pi Zero case camera lid, ensuring that you have the lid the right way round so it will shut! You can now twist the four cables for the Scroll pHAT HD together and cover them with a length of heat shrink. Be sure to leave yourself a bit of slack on these cables inside the case to allow you to open and close the lid. I used a little piece of Blu-Tack to affix the ADXL345 to the lid at this point so that I could be sure my cables were neatly aligned and in the correct place.

Once you are happy that your cables are in the right place, we need to glue the ADXL345 into the lid of our Pi Zero case in such a manner that we know which axis will be pointing up when we wear our pedometer. You can see in this picture that I have the ADXL345 at the bottom of the lid (with the Raspberry Pi logo at the bottom) with the x axis on the vertical if I were to stand my Pi Zero case on its end. You need to make sure that your ADXL345 is mounted in the same orientation or the following program will not function correctly:

We are now ready to test our hardware is communicating with our Pi Zero, and then to begin writing our Python program to count our steps.

Counting steps with Python

Power on your Pi Zero and connect to it via SSH as usual. If you have not followed the previous chapters in this book, then at this point, you may well need to enable the I2C protocol. Refer to the Chapter 2, *Scrolling LED Badge*, for details of how to do this.

With this covered, let's check whether we can talk to both devices on our I2C bus. Type the following into your Pi Zero:

```
sudo i2cdetect -y 1
```

All being well, you should see the following:

```
pi@wearablepi:~ $ sudo i2cdetect -y 1
     0  1  2  3  4  5  6  7  8  9  a  b  c  d  e  f
00:          -- -- -- -- -- -- -- -- -- -- -- --
10: -- -- -- -- -- -- -- -- -- -- -- -- -- -- -- --
20: -- -- -- -- -- -- -- -- -- -- -- -- -- -- -- --
30: -- -- -- -- -- -- -- -- -- -- -- -- -- -- -- --
40: -- -- -- -- -- -- -- -- -- -- -- -- -- -- -- --
50: -- -- -- 53 -- -- -- -- -- -- -- -- -- -- -- --
60: -- -- -- -- -- -- -- -- -- -- -- -- -- -- -- --
70: -- -- -- -- -- 74 -- -- -- --
pi@wearablepi:~ $
```

This lets us know that we have a device attached to the I2C bus on address 74 (our Scroll pHAT HD) and 53 (our ADXL345). If you cannot see both the devices on your I2C bus, shutdown your Pi Zero and check your soldering and cables. If we can see both the devices on the I2C bus, then we are ready to start writing some Python!

Graphing our steps

The first thing we are going to do is to write a short program, which will record our change in the *x* axis over time and record it into a file. We can then use this data to plot a graph, so we can decide on our threshold values.

Let's begin by installing the ADXL345 Python library into our project directory. Power on your Pi Zero and connect to it again via SSH. Once you are connected to your Pi Zero, create our new project directory by typing this:

```
mkdir ~/WearableTech/Chapter7
```

Then, move into that directory by typing this:

```
cd ~/WearableTech/Chapter7
```

As we did in Chapter 4, *A Motion-Reactive LED Cap*, we are now going to clone the Python library for the ADXL345 by typing this:

```
git clone https://github.com/jonwitts/adxl345-python.git
```

We can then move into the newly created directory by typing cd adxl345-python. We can now test our accelerometer is working by typing python3 example.py. You should see readings from your accelerometer scroll up the screen. If you hold your Pi Zero up so that the hole with the Scroll pHAT HD cable coming out is facing toward you and move it up and down, you should see the value of the *x* axis increase and decrease. This is what we want to graph. Press *Ctrl* + *C* together to stop the example.py program from running. Now, we will copy the adxl345.py library to our Chapter7 directory by typing this:

```
cd ../ && cp ./adxl345-python/adxl345.py ./
```

Type `nano stepGraph.py` to open Nano ready to write our program to record our change in the *x* axis to a file. In the Nano editor window which opens, type this program:

```
#!/usr/bin/python3

from adxl345 import ADXL345
from time import sleep
import csv

adxl345 = ADXL345()

with open('steps.csv', 'w', newline='') as csvfile:
    writer = csv.writer(csvfile, delimiter=',')
    for i in range(240):
        axes = adxl345.getAxes(True)
        writer.writerow([i + 1, axes['x']])
        sleep(0.125)
```

When you have typed this program, save it and close Nano by pressing *Ctrl* + *O*, then *Enter*, followed by *Ctrl* + *x*. What we are doing in this program is making use of Python's CSV library to allow us to write our accelerometer data out to a CSV file. After importing our libraries and creating our adxl345 object, we open a new CSV file called `steps.csv`. We then create our writer and set the field delimiter to be a comma. We now enter into a for loop, looping round 240 times. In each iteration of the loop, we get a current reading from our accelerometer, and then we will write a row to our CSV file containing the loop index, plus one followed by the current value of the *x* axis. Lastly, we sleep for an eighth of a second.

Before we run this program, we are going to need to attach our Pi Zero to ourselves and have a portable power source. If you have your Pi Zero plugged into the mains, shut it down and plug it into your portable power pack. Be sure to use a USB cable long enough, so you can put the power pack in your pocket and attach your Pi Zero to your clothing. Once you have powered your Pi Zero with a battery pack reconnect over SSH and move back into your the `Chapter7` directory.

We now need to fashion a way of attaching our Pi Zero and Scroll pHAT HD to ourselves, in such a way that we know the change in the x axis of the accelerometer is going to be inline with our up and down motion of our steps. I am using the same kind of sticky-backed badge pins that I used in the Chapter 2, *Scrolling LED Badge,* and have stuck one to the back of the Scroll pHAT HD again; and this time, I have stuck one to the back of my Pi Zero case, as you can see in this picture:

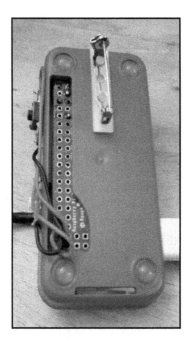

You can now pin the Pi Zero to your clothing, ensuring that the x axis of your accelerometer is aligned vertically. Pin your Scroll pHAT HD to your clothing too, and then pop your portable power pack into your pocket. Back on your SSH connection to your Pi Zero, type python3 ./stepGraph.py to start your program. You now have one minute to walk as naturally as possible, so we can capture the change in your x axis acceleration to our CSV file.

Once your program finishes running, you can sit down again and take off your Pi Zero! You can now have a look at the contents of this file by typing less steps.csv. You should see a file similar to this:

```
⊙ ⊙ ⊙     pi@wearablepi: ~/WearableTech/Chapter7
1,0.868
2,0.908
3,0.908
4,0.888
5,0.836
6,0.94
7,0.812
8,1.104
9,0.904
10,0.98
11,0.908
12,0.992
13,0.936
14,1.04
15,1.144
16,0.896
17,0.812
18,0.816
19,0.932
20,0.78
21,0.66
22,1.004
23,0.988
steps.csv
```

To close Less, press *q*. To represent this data in a graphical form, we really need to get it off the Pi Zero and onto our computer that we are working from. There are numerous packages out there, which will allow you to create a line graph from a CSV file, Excel probably being the most common, so I will not talk about how you create your graph.

To copy files from a headless Pi Zero setup over SSH, we need to use a program called SCP. On Linux and Mac OS X, the SCP program is available by default from your terminal window. On Windows, you are going to need to download another application to do this. For Windows, I find that WinSCP is the most user friendly. You can download it from `http s://winscp.net/eng/download.php`. Once installed, it will allow you to connect to your Pi Zero via either an IP address or a host name as you have been with SSH. You then get a familiar side-by-side windowed application to allow you to drag a file from the Pi Zero to a folder on your Windows computer.

If you are using Linux or Mac OS X, the command you will need to run from the terminal on your computer is this:

```
scp pi@wearablepi.local:/home/pi/WearableTech/Chapter7/steps.csv ./
```

You will be prompted to enter the password of your Pi Zero, and then your `steps.csv` file will be copied to the directory, which your terminal is opened in (your `home` folder by default).

You can now open this file in your favorite spreadsheet application, and create a line graph from the data. You want the first column to be the label for x axis for the graph, and if you make it produce a smooth line graph, you should see something like this:

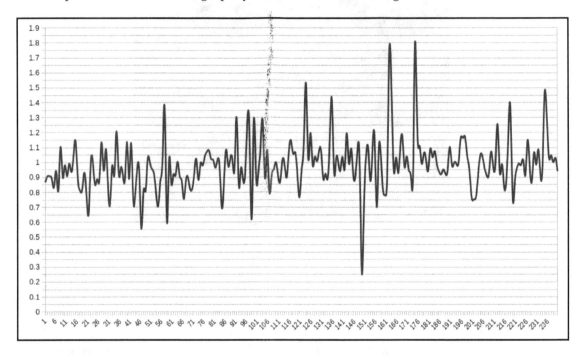

This is showing the change in the acceleration of the *x* axis of the accelerometer over a one minute period, as we walked about with our Pi Zero attached to us. We will use this graph to calculate our thresholds for starting to count a step and stopping counting a step in our next program. You will obviously need to adjust your program to match your data.

Based on the previous graph, we will start counting a step when the reading from the x axis goes above 1.15.

Creating our main program

We are now going to write our main Python program, which will run as soon as we turn on the Pi Zero and start to count our steps.

On your SSH connection to your Pi Zero, type the following to create your new Python file, `nano ~/WearableTech/Chapter7/pedCount.py`, and then copy this code into your file:

```python
#! /usr/bin/python3

# import our libraries
from adxl345 import ADXL345
from time import sleep
import scrollphathd as shd
from scrollphathd.fonts import font3x5

# setup our variables and objects
adxl345 = ADXL345()
pedCnt = 0
Thresh = 1.15 # Change this to match your threshold
last_state = 'below'

# define two functions to display messages
def scrollMsgOnce(msg):
    msg = msg + "      " # 6 spaces
    buffer = shd.write_string(msg, x=17, y=0, brightness=0.5)
    for i in range(buffer):
        shd.show()
        shd.scroll(1)
        sleep(0.05)
    shd.clear()
    shd.show()

def showMsgOnce(msg):
    shd.clear()
    shd.show()
    shd.write_string(msg, x=0, y=1, font=font3x5, brightness=0.25)
    shd.show()

# clear our screen and display a welcome message
shd.clear()
shd.show()
scrollMsgOnce("Raspberry Pi Zero Pedometer!")
sleep(0.5)

# start counting our steps
while True:
    # get our axes reading
    axes = adxl345.getAxes(True)
    # set current_sate - above or below
    # starts as below
    current_state = last_state
    if axes['x'] < Thresh:
```

```
        # we are still below threshold
        current_state = 'below'
    elif axes['x'] > Thresh:
        # we have gone above threshold
        current_state = 'above'

    if current_state is not last_state:
        # we have a change in state
        if current_state is 'above':
            # that change is to go above
            # so increment count and display it
            pedCnt += 1
            showMsgOnce(str(pedCnt))

    # set last state to current
    last_state = current_state
```

Save the file by pressing *Ctrl + O*, followed by *Enter*, and then exit Nano by pressing *Ctrl + X*. Now, we will make the file executable by typing this:

```
sudo chmod +x ./pedCount.py
```

There are comments throughout this program explaining what each step is doing. The only remaining things to do are to make our program run automatically and the to test out our pedometer!

Making our program run automatically

As with our previous projects, we now need to make our program start as soon as we switch our Pi Zero on.

First we will create our service definition file, so type this:

```
sudo nano /lib/systemd/system/pedCount.service
```

Now type the definition into it:

```
[Unit]
Description=Pedometer Service
After=multi-user.target

[Service]
Type=idle
ExecStart=/home/pi/WearableTech/Chapter7/pedCount.py

[Install]
```

```
WantedBy=multi-user.target
```

Save and exit Nano by typing *Ctrl* + *O*, followed by *Enter*, and then *Ctrl* + *X*. Now, change the file permissions, reload the `systemd` daemon, and activate our service by typing this:

```
sudo chmod 644 /lib/systemd/system/pedCount.service
sudo systemctl daemon-reload
sudo systemctl enable pedCount.service
```

Now, we need to test if this is working, so reboot your Pi by typing `sudo reboot`, and then when your Pi Zero restarts, you should see your Scroll pHAT HD scroll the message across the screen. Once you see the message scroll, you can then move your Pi Zero up and down through the *x* axis to see it count steps. If this is all working, press and hold your power-off button for 3 seconds to shut your Pi Zero down.

You can now pin your Scroll pHAT HD and Pi Zero to your clothing; put your portable power pack in your pocket; power up your Pi Zero, and then start counting your steps! If you find that your pedometer is wildly inaccurate, you can edit your threshold level in line 12 of the program to try and make it more accurate.

Summary

In this chapter, you learned about the complexities of creating an accurate pedometer by taking a look at some of the maths involved in this process too. We also saw how to chain multiple I2C devices together on our Pi Zero. To be able to calibrate our pedometer program, you had to learn how to write data to a CSV file using Python, and then we briefly looked at how we can copy those files from our Pi Zero to our main computer using the SCP protocol.

Our final program combined the use of the Scroll pHAT HD from the Chapter 2, *Scrolling LED Badge,* with the reading of the accelerometer data that we first looked at in the Chapter 4, *A Motion-Reactive LED Cap.*

In our next chapter, we are going to look at how we can use our Pi Zero to create a simple heart rate monitor.

8
Creating Your Own Heart Rate Monitor

In this project, we will make use of a Pulse Sensor Amped heart rate monitor, a Pimoroni Enviro pHAT, and a Pimoroni Scroll pHAT HD to create our own heart rate monitor, which will display our heart's BPM numerically and graphically on the Scroll pHAT HD.

If you are using the same Pi Zero for this project as you did for the previous project, desolder the six cables, which lead from the Pi Zero to the ADXL345 and Scroll pHAT HD, but leave your off switch and LED in place, as you may need to detach these from the case first. You will also need to desolder the cables to your Scroll pHAT HD as we will be reusing this; and remove the ADXL345 from the lid of your Pi Zero case. To deactivate the software running automatically, connect to your Pi Zero over SSH and issue the following command:

```
sudo systemctl disable pedCount.service
```

Once the command completes, you can shut down your Pi Zero by pressing your off switch for three seconds. Now, let's look at what we are going to cover in this chapter.

What we will cover

In this chapter, we will cover the following topics:

- Setting up our hardware
- Reading our heart rate
- Writing our main Python program
- Making our program run automatically

So, let's not hang about and take a look at what we will need to complete this project.

The bill of parts

We will make use of the following things in this project:

- A Pi Zero W
- An official Pi Zero Case
- A portable USB battery pack for your Pi Zero
- A Pulse Sensor Amped heart rate sensor
- A Pimoroni Enviro pHAT
- A Pimoroni Scroll pHAT HD
- 3 x 330 Ω resistors
- Stranded core cable—red, black, yellow, and blue
- Soldering iron and solder
- A hot glue gun

Setting up our hardware

The first thing we are going to do is to set up our pieces of hardware so that the Pi Zero can communicate with each piece correctly. The Pulse Sensor Amped is a 5V analog device designed for use with the Arduino products. Arduino boards have a builtin **Analog to Digital Converter** (**ADC**), which allows you to connect analog sensors and monitor them digitally. The Pi Zero does not have an ADC; this is where the Enviro pHAT comes in. We will use the ADC of the Enviro pHAT to connect our analog heart rate sensor to our Pi Zero and finally use the Scroll pHAT HD as our display system. There is one more problem, which we need to solve with this sensor; the problem is that it's output is at 5V and our Pi Zero and the Enviro pHAT wants the input at 3.3V. To achieve this, we are going to use a simple resistor-based voltage divider. We are going to use 3 x 330 Ω resistors to divide our voltage; one third will be directed off to a ground pin on the Pi Zero, and the remaining two thirds will be passed to our analog input on the Enviro pHAT.

This wiring diagram here shows you how we would wire this up using a breadboard:

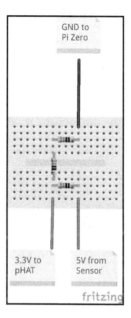

A breadboard is all well and good for testing things out, but we want to conceal all of our wiring into our Pi Zero case. To do this, we will solder our resistors and cables together in the same manner as this diagram, cutting any excess off, and then concealing it in the lid of our Pi Zero case. Here is a picture of how I have set up our voltage divider without the breadboard. The black cable will go back to ground pin on the Pi Zero, the purple cable is the 5V data cable from our Pulse Sensor Amped, and the blue cable will go to the 3.3V input on our ADC port of the pHAT:

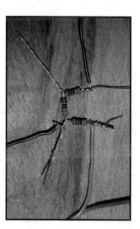

Solder each connection of your voltage divider, and then trim as much excess cable from each joint as you can. We will fit this into the lid of our Pi Zero case using hot glue to ensure that we do not get any shorts between the resistors. For now, we can just ensure that when testing things the resistors do not touch each other.

We are going to make use of the lid for the Pi Zero case, which has the long hole down it. Ensure that as you are wiring up and soldering your cable to the Pi Zero and your Enviro pHAT, you are feeding them through the hole in this lid in the correct manner or we will not be able to close everything up at the end of our project!

Here is the complete wiring diagram for our hardware:

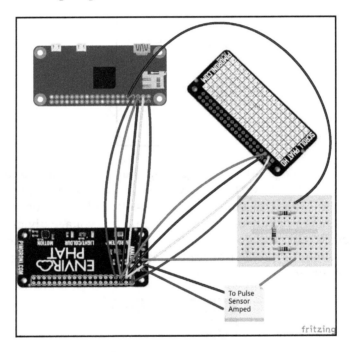

We are going to sit the Scroll pHAT HD directly on top of the Enviro pHAT, and then both of these will be glued to the lid of the Pi Zero Case. Cut yourself 10-12 cm of cable; and solder your connections between the Pi Zero and the Enviro pHAT. When you solder your cables to the Enviro pHAT, feed them up through the bottom of the pHAT and feed the cables into the Pi Zero from the top. You can trim the cable from GPIO4 that comes through the pHAT, but leave the other four standing proud of the pHAT, as we are going to feed these through the Scroll pHAT HD to attach it to the I2C bus directly on top of the other pHAT.

You can see in this picture that my Scroll pHAT HD sat on top of my Enviro pHAT, ready to be soldered to the four cables for the I2C bus:

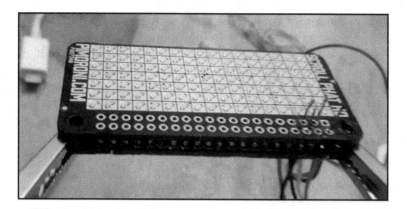

You can see that the two crocodile clips of my helping hand are holding the two pHATs apart, and you maybe able to see that I have used a small piece of Blu-Tack at the other side to stop the boards from touching. Once we have soldered the cables to the Scroll pHAT HD and snipped them, we will place four blobs of hot glue between the boards on each corner to stop any electrical shorts happening.

Once the glue has dried, and you are happy that the two boards will not be able to touch each other, we are going to stick the Enviro pHAT to the lid of our Pi Zero case with some more hot glue. Make sure that you line it up nice and centrally and that you have feed all your cables in through the hole in the lid. I am feeding the three cables back to my sensor back out of the hole in the lid just behind the top left of our pHATs, as you can see in this picture:

Now that we have secured our pHATs to our Pi Zero case lid, we need to secure our voltage divider into the underside of the lid. Turn your lid over and try to arrange your cables as neatly as possible. First, I applied a small amount of hot glue to the underside of the lid, close to where the sensor cables enter, and secured a loop of the three sensor cables and the blue cable going from the voltage divider to the Enviro pHAT. I then placed another spot of hot glue into the lid and pushed the voltage divider into it, ensuring that all three resistors where secured so that they could not touch each other. Just prior to doing this, I desoldered the blue cable from the voltage divider and cut it to length, and then resoldered it to the voltage divider. This meant that I did not have excess cable in the lid of my case. To finish off the cables in the lid, I placed another bit of hot glue and stuck the cables, which are connected to the Pi Zero to the lid to provide a bit of tension support when the lid is opened and closed.

You can see the finished cables and voltage divider in this picture:

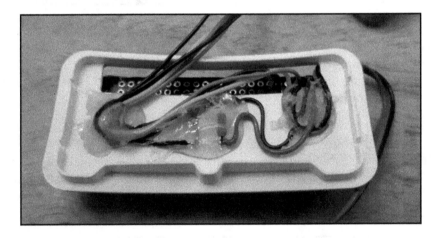

At this point, I took the opportunity to desolder the six cables coming from the pHATs to my Pi Zero, at the Pi Zero end; and shortened them as much as I could while still being able to safely solder them back to my Pi Zero. Once everything was resoldered and neatly closed inside the case, I stuck a sticky backed badge pin horizontally across the center of the back of the Pi Zero case so that we can attach it to our clothes whilst using it.

Reading our heart rate

Now that we have connected all of our hardware, we should first check whether we can see all of our devices on the I2C bus. Switch on your Pi Zero, and connect to over SSH. Once you are logged in, run the following command to check the devices detected on the I2C bus – `i2cdetect -y 1`. You should see the same as this:

```
pi@wearablepi:~ $ i2cdetect -y 1
     0  1  2  3  4  5  6  7  8  9  a  b  c  d  e  f
00:          -- -- -- -- -- -- -- -- -- -- -- -- --
10: -- -- -- -- -- -- -- -- -- -- -- -- -- 1d -- --
20: -- -- -- -- -- -- -- -- -- 29 -- -- -- -- -- --
30: -- -- -- -- -- -- -- -- -- -- -- -- -- -- -- --
40: -- -- -- -- -- -- -- -- -- 49 -- -- -- -- -- --
50: -- -- -- -- -- -- -- -- -- -- -- -- -- -- -- --
60: -- -- -- -- -- -- -- -- -- -- -- -- -- -- -- --
70: -- -- -- -- 74 -- -- 77
pi@wearablepi:~ $ 
```

This is telling us that we can see five different devices on our I2C bus:

- `0x49`: Enviro pHAT - ADS1015
- `0x29`: Enviro pHAT - TCS3472
- `0x1d`: Enviro pHAT - LSM303D
- `0x77`: Enviro pHAT - BMP280
- `0x74`: Scroll pHAT HD

If you cannot see these five devices on your I2C bus, then you need to go back and check whether your wiring matches the diagram and that your solder joints are all good.

We now need to install some pieces of software to interface with our hardware. Let's start with the software for the Enviro pHAT, type the following command:

```
curl -sS https://get.pimoroni.com/envirophat | bash
```

When asked if you want to continue, press *Y* followed by *Enter*. Notice the warning about this device using I2C. If you have not followed the previous chapters, then you will need to set up the I2C interface on your Pi Zero. Chapter 2, *Scrolling LED Badge*, tells you how to do this. When you are prompted about performing a full install, press *Y*, followed by *Enter*.

We are also going to make use of the Scroll pHAT HD as our display, so let's go ahead and install the software for that too by typing the following command:

```
curl https://get.pimoroni.com/scrollphathd | bash
```

Again, when prompted to continue, press *Y*, followed by *Enter*, and when asked if you would like to carry out a full install, press *Y* followed by *Enter* again.

We now have the necessary software installed to be able to monitor our heart rate and display the data on our Scroll pHAT HD. Let's get on with writing our program!

Our program will read the input from our analog heart rate sensor, which the Enviro pHAT reports as a voltage between 0-3.3V. We are looking to record the time between high peaks in the voltage to determine how many beats per minute our heart is beating at. First off, let's write a small program, which will let us see the rate rate monitor working. Make a new directory for our project and move into it by typing this:

```
mkdir ~/WearableTech/Chapter8 && cd ~/WearableTech/Chapter8
```

Now, create a new python program by typing this:

```
nano pulseTest.py
```

Type the following code into it:

```python
#!/usr/bin/python3

from envirophat import analog
from time import sleep

while True:
    pulse = analog.read(0)
    print("Pulse Voltage = {0}".format(pulse))
    sleep(0.25)
```

Save the file by pressing *Ctrl + O*, followed by *Enter*, and then exit Nano by pressing *Ctrl +* *X*. You can now attach your heart rate sensor to your finger using the supplied piece of velcro, and then run this program to see the voltage change with your pulse by typing `python3 ./pulseTest.py`. You should see an output similar to this:

```
pi@wearablepi: ~/WearableTech/Chapter8
Pulse Voltage = 1.807
Pulse Voltage = 1.897
Pulse Voltage = 1.534
Pulse Voltage = 1.45
Pulse Voltage = 1.816
Pulse Voltage = 2.077
Pulse Voltage = 1.492
Pulse Voltage = 1.396
Pulse Voltage = 1.93
Pulse Voltage = 1.768
Pulse Voltage = 1.423
Pulse Voltage = 1.336
Pulse Voltage = 1.348
Pulse Voltage = 2.425
Pulse Voltage = 1.552
Pulse Voltage = 1.45
Pulse Voltage = 1.552
Pulse Voltage = 2.959
Pulse Voltage = 1.531
^CTraceback (most recent call last):
  File "./pulseTest.py", line 9, in <module>
    sleep(0.25)
KeyboardInterrupt
pi@wearablepi:~/WearableTech/Chapter8 $
```

Press *Ctrl + C* to stop the program from running. Now that we know that we can read the data from our sensor, let's set out what our program will do before we dive into writing it. Create our main Python program file by typing nano `pulseRead.py`, and type the following code into the text editor. The code is commented well throughout to explain what is going on:

```
#!/usr/bin/python3

# based on
https://github.com/udayankumar/heart-rate-raspberry-pi/blob/master/heartBea
ts.py
# adapted for the Enviro pHAT

import time
import scrollphathd as sph
from scrollphathd.fonts import font3x5
from envirophat import analog

# define our scroll phat functions
# a large and small heart to animate
```

```
# display a number or message
def largeHeart(b):
    sph.clear_rect(0, 0, 6, 7)
    sph.show()
    sph.set_pixel(0, 0, b/2)
    sph.set_pixel(1, 0, b)
    sph.set_pixel(3, 0, b)
    sph.set_pixel(4, 0, b/2)
    sph.set_pixel(0, 1, b)
    sph.set_pixel(1, 1, b)
    sph.set_pixel(2, 1, b)
    sph.set_pixel(3, 1, b)
    sph.set_pixel(4, 1, b)
    sph.set_pixel(0, 2, b)
    sph.set_pixel(1, 2, b)
    sph.set_pixel(2, 2, b)
    sph.set_pixel(3, 2, b)
    sph.set_pixel(4, 2, b)
    sph.set_pixel(0, 3, b/2)
    sph.set_pixel(1, 3, b)
    sph.set_pixel(2, 3, b)
    sph.set_pixel(3, 3, b)
    sph.set_pixel(4, 3, b/2)
    sph.set_pixel(1, 4, b)
    sph.set_pixel(2, 4, b)
    sph.set_pixel(3, 4, b)
    sph.set_pixel(1, 5, b/2)
    sph.set_pixel(2, 5, b)
    sph.set_pixel(3, 5, b/2)
    sph.set_pixel(2, 6, b)
    sph.show()

def smallHeart(b):
    sph.clear_rect(0, 0, 6, 7)
    sph.show()
    sph.set_pixel(1, 1, b)
    sph.set_pixel(2, 1, b)
    sph.set_pixel(1, 2, b)
    sph.set_pixel(2, 2, b)
    sph.set_pixel(3, 2, b)
    sph.set_pixel(1, 3, b/2)
    sph.set_pixel(2, 3, b)
    sph.set_pixel(3, 3, b/2)
    sph.set_pixel(2, 4, b)
    sph.show()

def printBPM(b, msg):
    sph.clear_rect(6, 0, 11, 8)
```

```
    sph.write_string(msg, x=6, y=1, font=font3x5, letter_spacing=1,
brightness=b)
    sph.show()

# set up our pulse rate variables and constants
curState = 0
thresh = 1.65 #half of 3.3V
P = 1.0
T = 1.0
stateChanged = 0
sampleCounter = 0
lastBeatTime = 0
firstBeat = True
secondBeat = False
Pulse = False
IBI = 600
rate = [0]*10
amp = 100


lastTime = int(time.time()*1000)

while True:
    # read from the ADC
    Signal = analog.read(0)
    curTime = int(time.time()*1000)
    sampleCounter += curTime - lastTime
    lastTime = curTime
    N = sampleCounter - lastBeatTime # monitor the time since the last beat
to avoid noise
    ##  find the peak and trough of the pulse wave
    if Signal < thresh and N > (IBI/5.0)*3.0 : # avoid dichrotic noise by
waiting 3/5 of last IBI
        if Signal < T : # T is the trough
            T = Signal  # keep track of lowest point in pulse wave
            smallHeart(0.25) # measured a trough so show small heart

    if Signal > thresh and Signal > P: # thresh helps avoid noise
        P = Signal # P is the peak - keep track of highest point
        largeHeart(0.25) # measured a peak so show a large heart

    # signal surges up in value every time there is a pulse
    if N > 250 : # avoid high frequency noise
        if  (Signal > thresh) and  (Pulse == False) and  (N >
(IBI/5.0)*3.0)  :
            Pulse = True # set Pulse flag when we think a pulse
            IBI = sampleCounter - lastBeatTime # time between beats
            lastBeatTime = sampleCounter # keep track of time
```

```python
    if secondBeat : # if secondBeat == TRUE
        secondBeat = False # clear secondBeat flag
        for i in range(0,10): # running total to get
                             # a realisitic BPM at startup
            rate[i] = IBI;

    if firstBeat : # if firstBeat == TRUE
        firstBeat = False # clear firstBeat flag
        secondBeat = True # set the second beat flag
        continue # IBI value is unreliable so discard it

    # keep a running total of the last 10 IBI values
    runningTotal = 0 # clear the runningTotal variable

    for i in range(0,9): # shift data in the rate array
        rate[i] = rate[i+1] # and drop the oldest IBI value
        runningTotal += rate[i] # add up the 9 oldest IBI

    rate[9] = IBI # add the latest IBI to the rate array
    runningTotal += rate[9]  # + latest IBI to runningTotal
    runningTotal /= 10       # average the last 10 IBI
    BPM = 60000/runningTotal # how many beats can fit into a
                             # minute? that's BPM!
    printBPM(0.25, str(int(BPM))) # we have a BPM
                             # lets display it

if Signal < thresh and Pulse == True : # when the values are
                             # going down, the beat is over
    Pulse = False # reset the Pulse flag
    amp = P - T # get amplitude of the pulse wave
    thresh = amp/2 + T # set thresh at 50% of the amplitude
    P = thresh # reset these for next time
    T = thresh

if N > 2500 : # if 2.5 seconds go by without a beat
    thresh = 1.65 # set thresh default
    P = 1.0 # set P default
    T = 1.0 # set T default
    lastBeatTime = sampleCounter # lastBeatTime up to date
    firstBeat = True # set these to avoid noise
    secondBeat = False # when we get the heartbeat back
    printBPM(0.25, "-^-")

time.sleep(0.005)
```

Save the file by pressing *Ctrl + O*, followed by *Enter*, and then exit Nano by pressing *Ctrl + X*. Now, we will make the file executable by typing this:

```
sudo chmod +x ./pulseRead.py
```

All that is left to do is to make our program run automatically and test out our heart rate monitor!

Making our program run automatically

As with our previous projects, we now need to make our program start as soon as we switch our Pi Zero on.

First we will create our service definition file, so type this:

```
sudo nano /lib/systemd/system/pulseRead.service
```

Now, type the definition into it:

```
[Unit]
Description=Heart Rate Service
After=multi-user.target

[Service]
Type=idle
ExecStart=/home/pi/WearableTech/Chapter8/pulseRead.py

[Install]
WantedBy=multi-user.target
```

Save and exit Nano by typing *Ctrl + O*, followed by *Enter*, and then *Ctrl + X*. Now, change the file permissions, reload the systemd daemon, and activate our service by typing this:

```
sudo chmod 644 /lib/systemd/system/pulseRead.service
sudo systemctl daemon-reload
sudo systemctl enable pulseRead.service
```

Now, we need to test if this is working, so reboot your Pi by typing `sudo reboot;` and then when your Pi Zero restarts, place your finger upon your heart rate monitor, and you should see your Scroll pHAT HD start to animate your heart beats and display your heart rate. If this is all working, press and hold your power-off button for three seconds to shut your Pi Zero down.

You are now ready to power your Pi Zero from your portable power pack, and monitor your heart rate while you are out and about!

Summary

In this chapter, we saw how we can attach analog sensors to our Pi Zero with the use of an ADC, and how we can add 5V sensors to our 3.3V Pi Zero with the use of a simple resistor-based voltage divider. We have also gone a bit further with our use of the Scroll pHAT HD by creating two different areas on our display, which update at different intervals.

The program for monitoring our heart rate introduces some more advanced mathematics to keep a track of the high and low pulses of our sensor, tracking the time between them, and calculating the average of a set of ten of these beats to calculate our BPM.

You can see a video of my completed heart rate monitor at `https://www.youtube.com/watch?v=CaQMu6f1UJ8`

In our next and final chapter, we will create our own GPS tracker, which we can use to log where and how far we move, while we are out and about!

9
Creating Your Own GPS Tracker

In our final project, we will make a portable GPS tracker for bikers or walkers to use while out and about. The GPS tracker will log your GPS coordinates, including elevation and time. We will then also configure the Pi to create a file in the correct format to import into Google Maps or Google Earth.

If you are using the same Pi Zero for this project as you did for the previous project, desolder the six cables that lead from the Pi Zero to the Enviro pHAT and Scroll pHAT HD, but leave your off switch and LED in place, as you may need to detach these from the case first. You should also remove the cables and voltage divider from the lid of your Pi Zero case. To deactivate the software running automatically, connect to your Pi Zero over SSH and issue the following command:

```
sudo systemctl disable pulseRead.service
```

Once the command completes, you can shut down your Pi Zero by pressing your off switch for 3 seconds. Now, let's look at what we are going to cover in this chapter.

What we will cover

In this chapter, we will cover the following topics:

- Connecting up our hardware
- Configuring our Pi Zero to connect to the hardware
- Reading our GPS data
- Creating KML files

- Creating our final program
- Making our program run automatically
- Testing our GPS tracker

So first off, let's look at what parts we will need to create this project.

The bill of parts

We will make use of the following things in this project:

- A Pi Zero W
- An official Pi Zero Case
- A portable USB battery pack for your Pi Zero
- A long (60 cm) USB A to a micro USB cable
- An Adafruit Ultimate GPS Breakout v3 module
- Stranded core cable - red, black, yellow, and blue
- Soldering iron and solder
- A hot glue gun
- A sticky backed badge pin
- An Adfruit SMA to µFL adaptor cable (optional)
- An Adafruit GPS Antenna (optional)

Setting up our hardware

The first thing we should do is get all of our hardware set up so that we can start testing it and creating our program. We will begin by connecting our GPS module to our Pi Zero. Our GPS module is just too big to fit inside of our Pi Zero case lid, so we will be making use of the case lid which has the circular hole for the camera and attaching our GPS module to the lid of the case. With this in mind, cut a long enough length of red, black, yellow, and blue cable to wire your Pi Zero and GPS module together; about 10 cm should do the job.

Strip and tin each end of your four cables so that they are ready to connect to our boards. If you solder your cables to your GPS module first, you can feed them through from the back of the module, and then feed them through the front of the case lid.

The diagram here shows how to wire Pi Zero and the GPS module together:

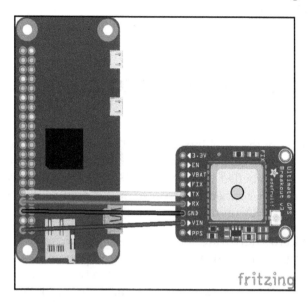

Once your cables are soldered to your GPS board and feed through the case lid, you can now solder them to your Pi Zero from the top of the board. Once you are happy with your solder joints and have checked that everything is connected as per the diagram, you can snip any excess cable off with side snips, and insert your Pi Zero into the base of the case. You can then twist the GPS module round a few times to neatly twist your four cables together and fit them into the lid. We are now going to attach the GPS module to the case lid with some hot glue. Try to line your GPS module up so that the cables enter straight into the lid. I had to have mine aligned slightly off center for this to work.

Here is a photo of my GPS module attached to my Pi Zero case:

To finish our hardware setup off, I placed a sticky-backed badge pin across the back of the case at the end with the GPS sensor attached. so I can fasten it to my clothing and have the GPS sensor able to *see* the sky.

Configuring our Pi Zero to connect to the hardware

You may have noticed from the labelling on the GPS module and from the pins that we connected the module to our Pi Zero on that we are using a serial device. The tell-tale sign for this was the TX and RX labelled pins on the GPS module board. You may also have noticed that we crossed these connections over to our Pi Zero; in that, we connected the TX from the GPS module to the RX on the Pi Zero and vice versa.

To make use of the Pi Zero's hardware serial pins, we need to make a number of changes to our software. The changes that are needed will depend upon whether you are using Pi Zero or Pi Zero W. The reason for the differences between the two editions of Pi Zero are because the Bluetooth added to Pi Zero W and Pi 3 boards make use of the serial port, so we need to take an extra step to stabilize our serial communications.

By default, the serial port is disabled, so we will use the `raspi-config` program to enable it and set a couple of things:

```
sudo raspi-config
```

In the menu which opens, select **5 Interfacing Options** and press **Enter**. In the next menu, highlight the **P6 Serial** item using your cursor keys and press *Enter*. You will then see the question shown as following. Select **No** and press *Enter*.

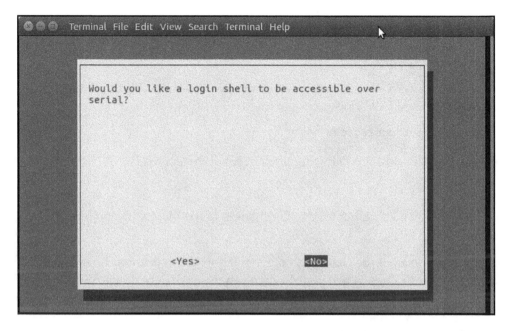

You will then be asked whether you want the serial port hardware to be enabled. Select **Yes** and press *Enter*. You will then be shown a confirmation such as this one; press *Enter* to close the serial port configuration tool:

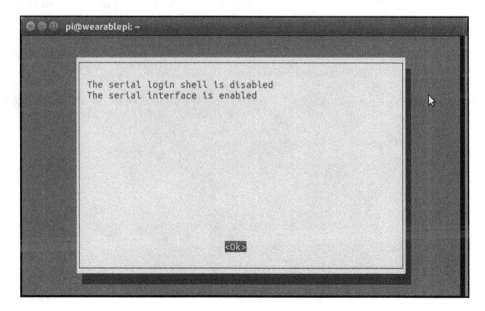

You will now be back on the main `raspi-config` menu. Press your *Tab* key twice to highlight **Finish** and press *Enter*. You will then be asked if you want to reboot, so select **No** and press *Enter*.

If you are using Pi Zero W (as I am), you will also need to make this final change to ensure that the Bluetooth and CPU clock does not interfere with our serial communication:

```
sudo nano /boot/config.txt
```

At the end of the file, add the following line if it is not there already:

```
enable_uart=1
```

Press *Ctrl* + *O* followed by *Enter* to save the changes to the file. Exit Nano by pressing *Ctrl* + *X*.

We have now made all of the changes to our serial port configuration. Type `sudo reboot now` to restart your Pi Zero. When your Pi Zero restarts, connect to it via SSH as usual.

Reading our GPS data

We need our GPS sensor to get a fix on the GPS satellites before we can read anything useful from it. You will know if this has happened as the small red *FIX LED* will start to flash once every 15 seconds instead of once every second. If you are running this indoors or are having difficulty getting a satellite lock, you can use the Adfruit SMA to μFL adaptor cable and Adafruit GPS Antenna, and put the antenna near or outside a window to get a satellite lock.

Now that we have a GPS satellite lock we can, at this point, just read the data coming from our GPS sensor by running this:

```
sudo cat /dev/ttyS0
```

If you all is well, you should something like this scrolling up your SSH terminal window:

```
pi@wearablepi: ~
$GPVTG,280.51,T,,M,0.03,N,0.05,K,D*30

$GPRMC,151320.000,A,5345.7752,N,00021.6992,W,0.04,274.47,090717,,,D*74
$GPVTG,274.47,T,,M,0.04,N,0.07,K,D*39
6992,W,0.04,274.47,090717,,,D*74
$GPGSA,A,3,27,08,07,11,18,21,10,16,15,26,,,1.12,0.82,0.76*0D

$GPRMC,151320.000,A,5345.7752,N,00021.6992,W,0.04,274.47,090717,,,D*74

$GPVG,274.47,T,,M,0.04,N,0.07,K,D*39

15,26,,1.06,0.75,0.75*00
◆^◆$GPRMC,151321.000,A,5345.7752,N,00021.6992,W,0.03,280.51,090717,,,D*7E
51320.000,A,5345.7752,N,00021.6992,W,0.04,274.47,090717,,,D*74

$GPVG,274.47,T,,M,0.04,N,0.07,K,D*39

15,26,,1.06,0.75,0.75*00
◆^◆$GPVTG,280.51,T,,M,0.03,N,0.05,K,D*30
6992,W,0.03,280.51,090717,,,D*7E
51320.000,A,5345.7752,N,00021.6992,W,0.04,274.47,090717,,,D*74

$GPVG,274.47,T,,M,0.04,N,0.07,K,D*39

15,26,,1.06,0.75,0.75*00
◆^◆$GPGGA,151322.000,5345.7752,N,00021.6993,W,2,11,0.75,2.1,M,47.0,M,0000,0000*7
F
```

Press *Ctrl* + *C* to exit the stream of GPS data. So our sensor is working and receiving data, but we need to be able to make use of this data in our programs. To do this, we now need to install some pieces of software. We will need to install some system packages and also another Python library. The system packages we will need are the gpsd package and the gps-clients package. Install them by typing this:

```
sudo apt-get install gpsd gpsd-clients python-gps -y
```

You may have noticed that the Python package is a Python 2 and not a Python 3 package. To date, there does not appear to be a functioning Python 3 version of this package, so we will make use of Python 2 for this project. Now that we have our required software, type the following command to create and move into our chapter working directory:

```
mkdir ~/WearableTech/Chapter9 && cd ~/WearableTech/Chapter9
```

Before we can read the GPS data, we need to adjust the gpsd package slightly. The gpsd package we installed a couple of steps ago installs a systemd service on our Raspberry Pi, which defaults to a local socket; however, we want to manually run our GPS software, and tell it which socket to listen to manually. Stop and disable the gpsd systemd service by typing this:

```
sudo systemctl stop gpsd.socket
sudo systemctl disable gpsd.socket
```

We can now manually run **gpsd** and point it to our GPS sensor by typing this:

```
sudo gpsd /dev/ttyS0 -F /var/run/gpsd.sock
```

After running this command, we can use the CGPS program to view the live data from our sensor. Type cgps -s, and you should see something similar to this:

Press *Ctrl* + *C* to stop CGPS from running; now, we are going to try writing a small Python program to display data from the GPS sensor. Start a new Python file by typing nano gpsTest.py and type the following code into it:

```
import gps

# taken from
https://learn.adafruit.com/adafruit-ultimate-gps-on-the-raspberry-pi?view=a
ll#using-your-gps

# Listen on port 2947 (gpsd) of localhost
session = gps.gps("localhost", "2947")
session.stream(gps.WATCH_ENABLE | gps.WATCH_NEWSTYLE)
```

```
while True:
    try:
        report = session.next()
        # Wait for a 'TPV' report and display the current time
        # To see all report data, uncomment the line below
        #print report
        if report['class'] == 'TPV':
            if hasattr(report, 'time'):
                print report.time
    except KeyError:
        pass
    except KeyboardInterrupt:
        quit()
    except StopIteration:
        session = None
        print "GPSD has terminated"
```

You can then save the program by pressing *Ctrl* + *O*, followed by *Enter*, and exit Nano by pressing *Ctrl* + *X*. Now, run your program by typing `python ./gpsTest.py`. You should see something like this scroll up your Terminal window:

Stop the program from running by pressing *Ctrl* + *C*. We now know that we can read our GPS data into Python, so we will move onto the next section where you will learn how to create files ready to be uploaded into Google Maps or Google Earth.

Creating KML files

A KML file is the file format that Google has developed and supports for transferring coordinate data into their Maps and Earth products. If we can convert our GPS data into a KML file, then we will be able to upload this into Google Maps and/or Google Earth to be able to view where we have been while using our GPS logger.

The library we shall use to create our KML files is called SimpleKML, and you install it by typing this:

```
sudo pip install simplekml
```

The documentation for this package is available at `https://simplekml.readthedocs.io/en/latest/`. Using the documentation available on this site, let's create a quick KML file, which has five readings from our GPS logger in it. Open a new file in Nano by typing `nano gpsKMLTest.py`, and type the following code into it:

```
import gps
import simplekml

session = gps.gps("localhost", "2947")
session.stream(gps.WATCH_ENABLE | gps.WATCH_NEWSTYLE)
kml = simplekml.Kml()

i = 0

try:
    while True:
        report = session.next()
        if report['class'] == 'TPV':
            if hasattr(report, 'lon'):
                gpsLon = report.lon
                if hasattr(report, 'lat'):
                    gpsLat = report.lat
                    if hasattr(report, 'alt'):
                        gpsAlt = report.alt
                        gpsName = "Test GPS Point {0}".format(i)
                        print gpsName
                        kml.newpoint(name=gpsName,
coords=[(gpsLon,gpsLat,gpsAlt)])
        i = i + 1

except KeyboardInterrupt:
    kml.save("gpsKMLTest.kml")
    quit()
```

Save the changes by pressing *Ctrl + O,* followed by *Enter,* and then exit Nano by pressing *Ctrl + X.* Before we run this file, let's just talk through what we are doing as this will form the basis of our final program.

Firstly, we import the `gps` and `simplekml` libraries, we then connect to our `gps` socket, and create a `simplekml` object called `kml`. Just before we enter our infinite while loop, we create a counter variable and set it to `0`.

We wrap our while loop inside a try and except error catching loop, which listens for a `KeyboardInterrupt` *(Ctrl + C)*; and when it hears that key press, we save the KML file and then quit.

If we step into the while loop to look at what is happening in this part of the program, first we create a report object and tell it to step into the next section of the session stream (`report = session.next()`). We then check whether our report object contains a TPV attribute; if it does, we then check for a longitude attribute; then we check for a latitude reading, and finally we check for an altitude reading. If all four of these values are found, we create a new KML point and assign the coordinate data we have just found to it. If we do not find any of those four values, we jump to the end of the loop where we increment our counter variable and go back to the beginning.

Run the file for a short while by typing `python ./gpsKMLTest.py`. Once it has run for about 10 seconds, and you have seen a number of `Test GPS Point` names be printed to the SSH Terminal, press *Ctrl + C* to interrupt the program. At this point, Python will create our KML file.

Uploading KML files to Google Maps and Earth

We can now upload these files into Google Maps and Google Earth, but first, we will need to get them off the Pi Zero. We will use SCP again to copy it from our Pi Zero to our main computer. `Chapter 7`, *Creating Your Own Pedometer,* detailed the use of SCP for copying files in more detail, including using WinSCP to copy from your Pi Zero to your Windows computer. For Linux and Mac users, you can issue a command similar to this in your local computer's terminal window:

```
scp pi@wearablepi.local:/home/pi/WearableTech/Chapter9/gpsKMLTest.kml
~/Desktop
```

Once you have the file copied to your local computer, we can upload it to Google Maps and Google Earth for it to plot out our GPS data for us. Let's look at Google Maps first.

Uploading KML files to Google Maps

First, visit `https://www.google.com/maps`, and make sure you are logged in with a Google account. Click on the three horizontal lines in the top-left corner to open the menu. From the Maps menu, select **Your Places,** and then the **MAPS** tab. Now, at the bottom of the Maps menu, click on the **Create map** link. A new untitled map window will open with a menu shown like this one:

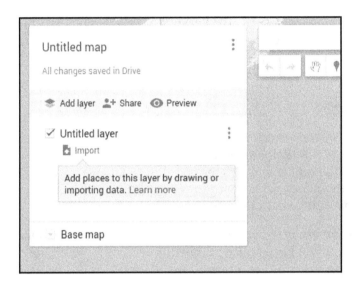

To import your KML file, click the blue **Import** link. You can then either upload your KML file. Upload the file you just copied from your Pi Zero. Your map should reload, and you should see the points you saved into your KML file with your Python program as points on the Google Map.

Uploading KML files to Google Earth

We can also upload our KML files into Google Earth to see the route we have travelled. Visit `https://earth.google.com/web/` again, ensuring that you are logged in with your Google account. Click on the three horizontal bars in the top-left corner of the browser window to open the Google Earth menu page. Click on the cog icon to open the settings window. At the bottom of the settings window is an option to enable the import of KML files; make sure this is switched on like so:

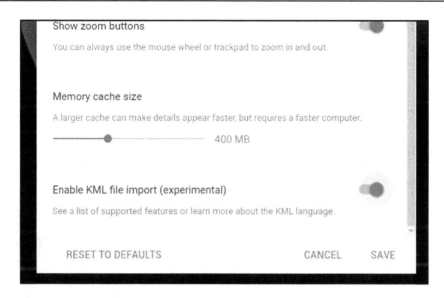

Now, click on **SAVE** to return to Google Earth. Now, click on the three horizontal lines again to reopen the menu, and this time click on the **My Places** menu item. You will now have an **Import KML File** option at the top of the menu which opens. Click on the **Import KML File** and select **Open file...** from the drop-down menu, as shown here:

Browse to the file you saved earlier and upload it. You should be zoomed straight into Google Earth at the point your GPS readings were taken from.

So now that we know that we can create KML files in a format that is compatible with Google Maps and Google earth, let's get straight on with writing our main program.

Creating our final program

As our main program needs to run as soon as we switch our Pi Zero on, and we are also not likely to have a remote connection to it while using it, we need to adjust what we have done so far a little.

Firstly, our program will need to set up the socket connection between our GPS module and the gpsd daemon. Secondly, we will not be able to pass a keyboard interrupt to stop this program running, so we will need another method of doing so. The most logical method seems to make use of the shutdown button and LED we added in Chapter 2, *Scrolling LED Badge*.

Create a new Python file, open it in Nano by typing nano ~/WearableTech/Chapter9/gpsTracker.py, and then copy the following program into it:

```python
#!/usr/bin/python

import gps
import simplekml
from gpiozero import Button, LED
from os import system
from time import sleep

# first create our gpsd socket
system("sudo killall gpsd")
system("sudo gpsd /dev/ttyS0 -F /var/run/gpsd.sock")

# now we create our connection to gpsd
session = gps.gps("localhost", "2947")
session.stream(gps.WATCH_ENABLE | gps.WATCH_NEWSTYLE)

# create our SimpleKML object
kml = simplekml.Kml()

# create our stop button and LED
stop_btn = Button(21, hold_time=3)
stop_led = LED(16)
```

```
# Define a function to stop the logger
def stopTracker():
    # flash our LED for half a second
    stop_led.on()
    sleep(0.5)
    stop_led.off()
    # create our filename stripping colon characters
    lineName = "gpsKML-{0}-{1}".format(firstTime, gpsTime).replace(":",
"-")
    # create our kml line object
    linestring = kml.newlinestring(name=lineName)
    # pass our compiled lineCoords to the new line object
    linestring.coords = lineCoords
    # set the altitude mode to clampedToGround
    linestring.altitudemode = simplekml.AltitudeMode.clamptoground
    # save our file
    kml.save("/home/pi/WearableTech/Chapter9/" + lineName + ".kml")
    # signal the loop to stop
    global stopLoop
    stopLoop = True
    # shutdown the pi
    system("sudo shutdown now -hP")

# do this if we hold the button for 3 sec
stop_btn.when_held = stopTracker

# wait for this to change to True
# i.e. when button pressed for 3 sec
stopLoop = False
# create an empty list for our coordinates
lineCoords = []
# set firstTime to empty string
firstTime = ""

while stopLoop != True:
    report = session.next()
    if report['class'] == 'TPV':
        if hasattr(report, 'time'):
            gpsTime = report.time
            if firstTime == "":
                # This is the first time reading update the variable
                firstTime = gpsTime
            if hasattr(report, 'lon'):
                gpsLon = report.lon
                if hasattr(report, 'lat'):
                    gpsLat = report.lat
                    if hasattr(report, 'alt'):
                        gpsAlt = report.alt
```

```
# add our 3 variables into the coordinates tuple
coordsTup = (gpsLon, gpsLat, gpsAlt)
# append our current tuple to our list
lineCoords.append(coordsTup)
```

Save the file by pressing *Ctrl + O* followed by *Enter* and exit Nano by pressing *Ctrl + X*.

What have just done is to initiate the socket connection to our GPS module in lines 10 and 11. Then in lines 21 through 44 we create a connection to our LED and button used to switch off the Pi Zero and then create a function which will finalize our KML file if the button is held for 3 seconds and then shutdown the GPS Tracker. We also program a visual indication of this by flashing the LED on for half a second. The remainder of the program is very similar to our KML test file from earlier, except we use a while loop, which checks the value of our `stopLoop` variable, and we are creating a KML Line object rather than placeholders. It is worth noting that in our `stopTracker` function, we had to make our `stopLoop` variable global so that the main while loop could see it too.

Making our program run automatically

One of our last steps here is to make this Python program run automatically. First, we need to make the program we just wrote executable by typing `sudo chmod +x ./gpsTracker.py`. Now, will create our service definition file by typing this:

sudo nano /lib/systemd/system/gpsTracker.service

Now, type the definition into it:

```
[Unit]
Description=GPS Tracker Service
After=multi-user.target

[Service]
Type=idle
ExecStart=/home/pi/WearableTech/Chapter9/gpsTracker.py

[Install]
WantedBy=multi-user.target
```

Save and exit Nano by typing *Ctrl + O*, followed by *Enter*, and then *Ctrl + X*. Now reload the systemd daemon and activate our service by typing this:

```
sudo systemctl daemon-reload
sudo systemctl enable gpsTracker.service
```

As we have combined the function of our Shutdown button into this Python program, we can now also stop that service from running by typing this:

```
sudo systemctl disable shutdownPi.service
```

Now, we need to test if this is working, so reboot your Pi by typing `sudo reboot`; and then when your Pi Zero restarts, wait for your GPS module to get a lock (the *FIX LED* flashes once every 15 seconds), give it 10 seconds, and then press and hold the power-off button for three seconds. You should see the LED flash on for just half a second and your Pi Zero should then shut down.

You are now ready to power your Pi Zero from your portable power pack while walking or cycling around and have it log your GPS position. You can then copy your KML files off your Pi Zero and upload them to either Google Maps or Earth to see your route taken.

Testing our GPS tracker

So, with your code all confirmed as working, it is time to pin your tracker to your top (try to make sure the ceramic aerial has a clear view of the sky), and go for a walk or ride. You should quite quickly see the *FIX LED* get a connection. Once you do see the FIX indication you know that your tracker is logging away for you.

When you finish the route you want to log, just press and hold your power-off button to switch everything off. When you return home you can copy the KML files off your Pi Zero as before and upload them into Google Maps or Google Earth to share your routes!

Here is an example of a route tracked with my Pi Zero GPS tracker seen in Google Earth:

Summary

In this chapter, we attached a serial device to our Pi Zero and configured the hardware serial port on the Pi Zero to allow us to communicate with it. We then looked at a number of ways we could read the data coming over the serial port, from reading the raw data to sending it into a specific program. We finally looked at using that data stream in our Python programs.

You learned about the SimpleKML program and how we can use this to create files of our GPS data, which we can easily upload into Google Maps or Google Earth to visualize the GPS data we are logging.

We finally pulled this all together into an automated program, which will run headless. It will enable us to start and stop our GPS tracking whenever we want by saving the logs to our Pi Zero ready for us to upload them to our mapping service when we return home.

Index